AF327171

TWO ON THE TRAIL

~a thousand miles on the PCT~

Ann Marshall

WASHINGTON TRAILS ASSOCIATION

Published by
Washington Trails Association
16812 36th Avenue West
Lynnwood Washington 98037

Photos by Lee Mc Kee

Cover: at the United States/Canada border
Back: top—near Methow Pass in the North Cascades
        center—near Stampede Pass, Washington
        bottom—Mount Jefferson, Oregon

ISBN 0-936289-01-5

Copyright © 1985 by Washington Trails Association
All rights reserved.

CONTENTS

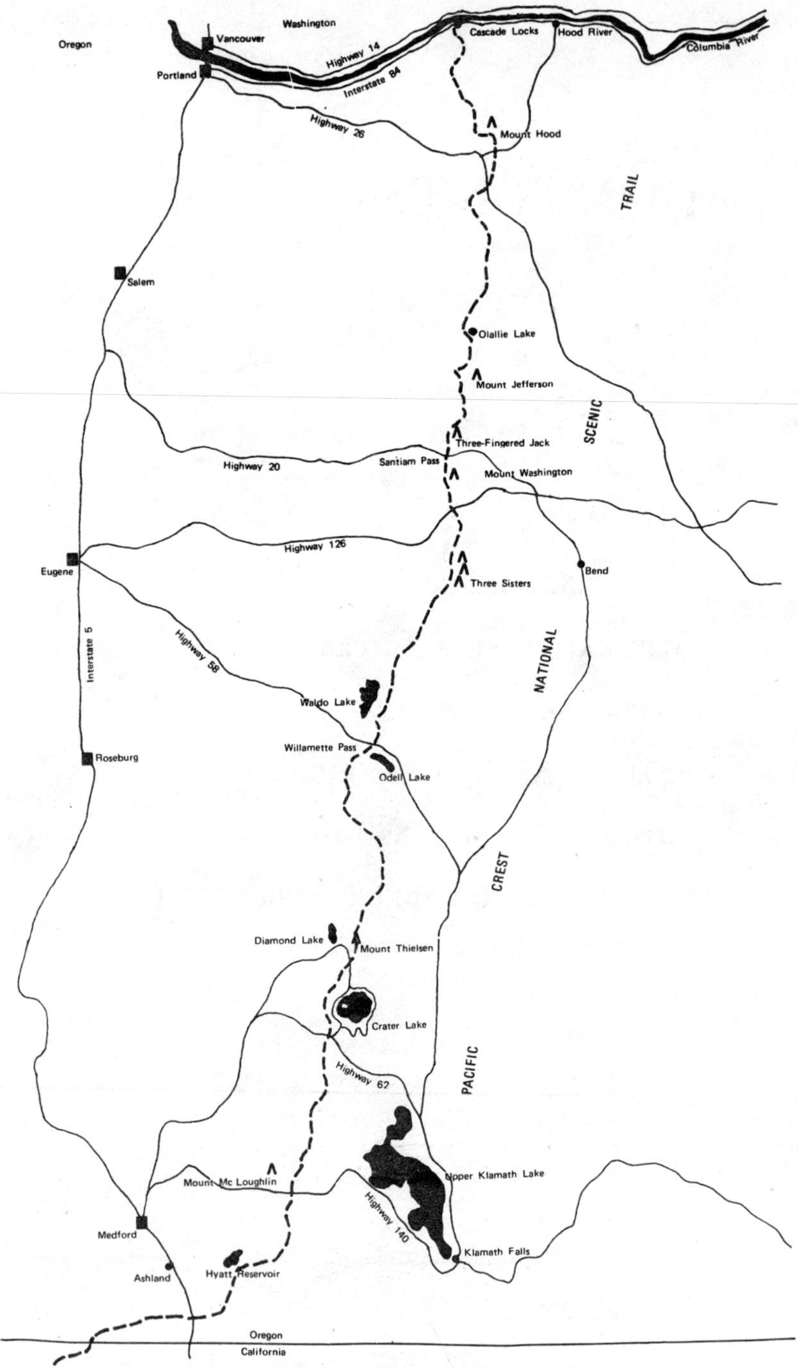

The PACIFIC CREST TRAIL in Oregon

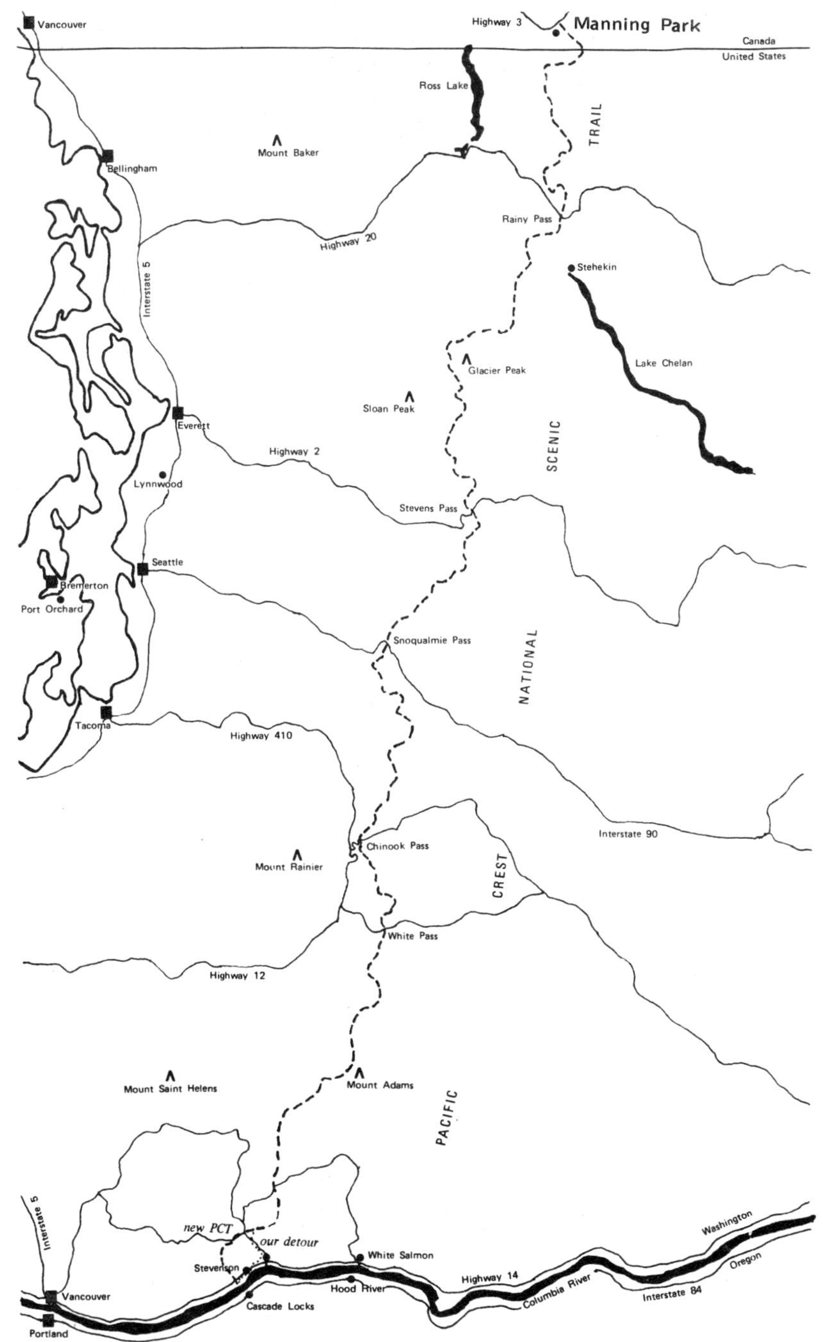

The PACIFIC CREST TRAIL in Washington

THE JOURNEY BEGINS

This is the story of how my partner and I—two hikers in our mid-thirties—left our homes and jobs to walk one thousand miles through the mountains of Oregon and Washington on the Pacific Crest Trail.

Lee and I spent about half a year planning and packing for this journey. We had talked about it for months, and each of us had had our own private dreams about hiking the PCT for years before that.

Although I had hiked bits and pieces of the PCT at times during my hiking "career," Lee had actually set out in 1978 to hike from Canada to Mount Hood. But after two weeks of rain, he was beaten; at Stevens Pass he ended his trip and went home. This would be his chance to cancel that failure.

Why on earth would a person *want* to walk a thousand miles through the Cascade Mountain Range? For an undertaking of this sort, no simple answer presents itself.

Lee and I both enjoy the feeling of setting off into the mountains with just our backpacks and our good sense to sustain us. We both find relaxation and excitement in leaving civilization behind us; we welcome the clarity of mind, the self-confidence, and the immersion into the natural rhythm of daylight and dark that come with spending time away from modern conveniences. We were tempted by the challenge of the long hike, knowing that if we succeeded, we would carry the sense of that accomplishment with us all of our lives.

At times our journey was very difficult; at other times we had lots of fun. And the entire trip was an adventure and an enrichment of our lives that could never have come to us otherwise. We realized that it would provide us with an intangible satisfaction that we needed to keep our lives on an even keel.

PACIFIC CREST TRAIL

From the Mexican border to Manning Provincial Park in British Columbia, the Pacific Crest National Scenic Trail stretches 2560 miles; our thousand-mile trip covered less than half the entire distance!

Now fifty years of age, in its early years the PCT was simply bits and pieces of pathway joined by dusty roads. Over the years it has become a full-fledged hikers' thoroughfare through rugged and demanding wilderness.

Its condition has been aided by the passage in 1968 of the National Trails System Act, which, among other things, made the Pacific Crest Trail one of the first two National Scenic Trails.

The National Trails System Act provided for a citizens' Advisory Council to help determine how all those bits and pieces should be joined. The Act has provided needed protection from trail-obliterating logging and road-building activities; the Council has made many improvements in the route.

However the Act also decreed that the Trail should remain on or near the *crest* of the mountain ranges through which it passes. The expensive re-routing to meet this requirement often takes hikers away from low-land water sources and protected camps to lead them into country that can be snowbound well into the summer.

GETTING READY

First, Lee and I made the decision to start at the Oregon/California border and hike to the northern terminus of the trail in Manning Provincial Park, British Columbia. Our subsequent preparations took many months. We studied maps and guidebooks. We read accounts of others' journeys, and we talked with people who had hiked the Trail.

We realized that we might be forced to take alternate routes because of snow or other weather conditions; we would have to carry the tools needed to locate and negotiate any alternate routes: good maps and a compass—and, more importantly, the knowledge of how to use those tools. Maps and compass are just two of the several essential items that all hikers routinely carry.

We outfitted ourselves with gear that would help protect us from the weather and terrain we would be crossing. Our equipment had to be versatile: we would encounter high volcanic plains, parched desert, rangeland, forested river valleys, snow-covered alpine passes, streams with no bridges; ice, mud, volcanic ash, rain, wind, cold and heat.

What if one of us were injured? Our survival might depend on what the other person knew. Together, we took a Mountaineering First Aid Class, and assembled a small emergency medical kit.

Worried about the possibility of ingesting *giardia lamblia*, a water-borne parasite, we decided to treat all our drinking water with an iodine solution. It was a wise decision, as we often did not have a *choice* of water sources and had to drink whatever we came across. Our conscientiousness paid off, as neither of us had intestinal difficulties.

Our shelter for the entire two and a half months was a 9'x11' coated nylon tarp. I sewed three nylon net panels that attached with Velcro strips to three sides of the tarp; this would be our mosquito protection. Tarp camping is not for everyone: it takes a lot of practice to set one up efficiently, and to get used to sleeping in it. But it worked well for us, giving us lots of room and allowing good air circulation. For supplemental protection, we each took a Gore-tex "bivvy bag," a waterproof protective covering for our sleeping bags.

In our thousand miles, we would have eight supply points at which we would pick up boxes that we had prepared ahead of time and mailed to ourselves. They would contain the next week-to-ten-days' food, film, maps and personal items.

The PCT crosses many major highways. Several of these crossings have stores, ranger stations, or resorts whose operators are quite willing to hold mail for PCT hikers. Fortunately, all of our boxes arrived at their destinations on time and in good condition, although we heard stories of other hikers who were not so lucky.

From our many years of hiking experience, we already owned nearly everything we needed. However, I decided to replace some of my worn equipment, and began the journey with a new pack and new boots. When loaded and ready to go, my pack weighed a horrifying 55 pounds!

Lee decided that his current pack and boots would be adequate, although he also bought several new items especially for the trip. Loaded and ready to go, Lee's pack weighed about 65 pounds!

We would not have enjoyed the trip as much without some "toys" along, even though they added weight to our packs. We each carried a camera, with an assortment of lenses, filters and gadgets. We each carried our own fishing outfits. Lee fished whenever he had the chance; I fished when conditions were right and the spirit moved me, which was not so often.

We each kept a private journal to record our individual experiences, and we kept a joint trail log to record distances, times and trail conditions. Excerpts from our journals make up the greater part of the tale that follows, as first one and then the other of us carries the story, with narration in between by me.

THE JOURNEY BEGINS...

We allowed ten weeks for the hike—a long time to be gone when you leave job, house, cats and family behind. Lee had to arrange a special leave from his position as an engineer at the Puget Sound Naval Shipyard in Bremerton. I had to arrange for someone in my office to continue to meet my publication deadlines for Signpost Magazine, for which I am editor. We each found people to look after our houses. We contacted friends in Medford, Janet Garner and Rex Bakel, who agreed to provide transportation to the trailhead for us.

We drew up lists of equipment and lists of things to do. We had menu lists and map lists and first-aid-equipment lists and clothing lists and a day-by-day itinerary. We saw lists in our dreams and at times it seemed that all we were doing was *planning*—that we would never get enough done to actually begin.

As our departure date drew near, we paid close attention to weather reports. Friends in southern Oregon warned that the winter snowpack was melting very slowly, that we might have difficulty just driving to our chosen trailhead, and that we would surely have trouble crossing such high spots as the Devil's Peak/Lee Peak saddle in the Sky Lakes Wilderness. We worried and fretted.

On July 17th, 1983, two days after my 35th birthday, the journey began ...

CALIFORNIA BORDER TO CRATER LAKE

JULY 17

Log: 7.1 miles, from Oregon/California border to Wrangle Camp. Skies overcast, temperatures cool, wind light.

Lee's journal: Last Friday, two days ago, was really the beginning of this journey, although looking back, those two days were hectic and stressful: leaving the shipyard, stopping at the bank to get travellers' checks and to leave last-minute items in the safe deposit box—I felt I was covering my tracks behind me as I ended my civilized life and began my journey life.

On Saturday there was the long drive to Medford in a rented car, which included several detours along the way—breakfast at my folks' house in Vancouver, a stop at the Portland Co-op for Ann's reel, a visit with Don and Dee Hinton in Rogue River, and finally trying to sleep in a stuffy motel room in Medford. My back has been in knots from tension.

But all that is over now. We are on the Trail. All the months of planning, scheduling, buying and packing are over. Now it is time to fulfill the commitment. That is the scary part. I don't want to fail this time as I did in 1978.

It is a challenge similar to a marathon run: you train, you plan, you pray, and you go for it, hoping everything falls into place and you make it to the end.

Ann's journal: As we headed for the trailhead this morning with Janet and Rex, we wondered how much snow we would find, and if we'd even be able to reach the trailhead. Reports from the Forest Service, from Janet, and from Lee's friend Don were not encouraging.

But we drove miles and miles without seeing even a patch of snow. The PCT crossing was right where the maps said it would be. Unloading packs, we scouted the trail briefly, took photos, and said good-byes and thank-yous.

Lee and I left our packs on the north side of the road and walked south with just cameras to find the official Oregon/California border. In about a quarter-mile we spotted a big sign mounted on a tree: "Oregon-California." This was it! Even though I had left home two days ago, this spot marked the actual *beginning* of our journey.

Lee's journal: The pack felt heavy today and my back is not 100 per cent okay, but I made it through the day. I am concerned at the weight

Our journey begins...

The official starting point.

Ann is carrying; it seemed to "tell" when she adjusted her pack, and it especially told on our pace —about five hours to cover the 6.6 miles to Wrangle Gap. We did lose the trail at times and snow made some stretches difficult, but the pace was too slow if we expect to hike 15 to 18 miles a day. Perhaps I will take some of the items in her pack tomorrow.

Ann's journal: I knew my pack would be heavy, but I was not prepared for how loaded-down I would feel with it on the trail. The load bore down on my shoulders so that I felt my lungs couldn't expand enough to breathe; my whole upper back ached, and my shoulder hurt. I felt unbalanced and not at all comfortable. My pace was about a mile an hour, which discouraged me. We can't do 18 miles a day at that rate.

Thus was our thousand-mile journey begun. As we set out for our first night's camp, we ascended Observation Peak, 7340 feet, and discovered that, yes indeed, there was snow here. The views were good from that elevation, and the open meadows were covered with flowers: paintbrush, larkspur, phlox, mariposa lily, stonecrop, blue-eyed grass, and more.

But after struggling to stay on the snow-covered trail, we decided to take the alternate route on a snow-covered *road,* which was easier to find and follow.

By the time we got to Wrangle Gap, wind was swirling clouds around us. We were the only people at the camp, about half a mile below Wrangle Gap.

> *Lee's journal:* **A** fire in the fireplace of the stone shelter here makes a fitting touch to the end of the first day. We started easy, the weather co-operated, and Wrangle Camp is perfect for our first night.

> *Ann's journal:* It is getting dark and a fog has sifted right down through the trees. I've got a crackling fire going in the fireplace. Lee is sitting next to me, also writing in his book. We have made it to the first camp on our journey; about seventy more to go. In spite of sore shoulders and back, I am looking forward to tomorrow's hike and the new country.

Our "perfect" campground lasted until sometime in the dead of night. I heard a noise. My eyes popped open. Lee still slept. I heard it again—loud, strange, and unnerving. I nudged Lee awake. When he got up to investigate, the noise stopped. It wasn't a noise that either one of us could place, and it was scary not to know what it was. A deer pawing the ground? By starlight, we could see a deer near the shelter, but she was calmly grazing—not likely the source of the noise.

Every time we heard the scraping, grinding noise, one of us would walk around with a light to try to find its source — but the noise would stop. After an hour of this, I *sneaked* out of my bag and *crept* to the nearest window. The noise continued and was very close. By chance, I shined the light up to the ceiling, and there, not five feet away from me, was a monster porcupine gnawing vigorously on a rafter!

(We should have known better, with all our experience, than to camp in a shelter. These backcountry buildings always are inhabited by "critters.")

We got up, lit the fire again, and wondered what to do. It was now three in the morning. We were dead tired, cold, and uneasy. We knew we wouldn't be able to sleep in the shelter with the porcupine gnawing away, so Lee went out into the black night to look for a spot to set up a sleeping place.

In a minute he called to me, and pointed out bright lights floating in the distance. In our spooky state of mind, we thought we were seeing a space station! We heard strange metallic clankings and even voices as our imaginations went

The shelter at Wrangle Camp.

to work in this unfamiliar country.

We went back by the fire and tried to calm ourselves. How could two experienced hikers get in a fix like this? Applying logic, we looked at a map and reasoned that our space station was simply the lights of Medford; the clanking was just the breeze blowing through a weather station not far from us. And the voices? Just our imaginations.

As we re-arranged our sleeping quarters outside and drifted back to sleep, we could hear the porcupine begin his frightful gnawing inside the shelter again.

JULY 18

Log: 11.5 miles, from Wrangle Camp to Mount Ashland Campground. Weather hot with strong winds.

> *Lee's journal:* It felt good to have daylight come so that my imagination could be put back in its place. We vowed never again to sleep in a shelter.
>
> Hiking today was on Road 20 since we are concerned about walking the trail with its snowdrifts. The guidebook gives Road 20 as an alternate to the PCT.

I took some of the food so Ann's pack would be a little lighter. We did well for the first four or five miles, then the weight of the pack, the sore shoulders and hips, and the unending climbing of the road began to take their toll.

Ann's journal: We weren't on the trail this morning until almost 10am. Boy, were my shoulders sore from yesterday! By mid-day we faced a long uphill pull of three miles from Siskiyou Gap. I began to run out of steam. Lee would go ahead, then wait for me every now and then. I felt badly for holding him back to my pace, as he could go much faster on his own. He didn't complain however—at least not out loud.

Our path was blocked with huge drifts of snow.

Lee's journal: The last several miles today were hard on both of us. My problem is the pack waist belt bruising my hips, plus the sore back I had before the trip started. I adjusted the belt tonight by raising it a notch on the frame in the hope that it will ride on a different spot and make tomorrow bearable.

We must hike 18½ miles tomorrow to reach a suitable campsite. Are we up to the distance? There's also a possibility of rattlesnakes since we will be dropping in elevation to cross Interstate 5.

We discussed our choices for several days from now, when we will be going over Devil's Peak. Don Hinton had suggested an alternate route because of the possibility of lots of snow remaining on the slopes—and me with no ice axe!

For tonight we should be comfortable; no porcupines in the rafters here. The camp is not as remote as Wrangle Gap; several cars have gone by. A fire snaps and crackles as we both write.

With all the aches and pains and concerns, it does feel good to be out here. Being with Ann is enjoyable. Besides fire-building, she does a good job of pouring water while I wash up!

This day's distance totalled almost twelve miles: five more than we had hiked on the first day. For not having slept well the night before, we managed alright on the hot and dusty road we were following as an alternate to the snowbound Pacific Crest Trail. Sometimes even the road was blocked by huge drifts of snow. These we would scale, then locate the road again.

On this second day, we crossed the Willamette Meridian. The sign marking the spot was dismantled, so we each propped up the sign to have our pictures taken with it.

JULY 19

Log: 19 miles, from Mount Ashland Campground to "Fenced-In Spring." Weather hot with strong wind on exposed slopes. No drinking water.

My only entry for the day read: "Cold and tired. Blistered feet. Grouchy and cranky. I'm going to bed."

Lee, however, described the day in slightly more detail:

Lee's journal: We didn't make it to our expected

camp by about 2.1 miles; however, it appears that
we did hike over 18 miles due to a mileage error
in the guidebook. Today's travels were over a mixture
of trail and road. We chose to walk Road 20 from
Ashland Campground all the way to Highway 99,
since we were not sure how well the trail was maintained on the lower new section. But because of the
hot, hard pavement and our heavy packs, we both
had developed blisters by the time we crossed under
I-5, and the remaining walk to camp was long and
tiring—could even be called miserable.

We are both tired tonight. We even got a little
short with one another at times. Clouds have settled
in with some accompanying thunder and drizzle—the
first rain of the trip.

The section of PCT we hiked today is fairly new, having
been completed only recently. It crosses BLM land that is
used mostly for range animals and is criss-crossed with jeep
trails. We found the PCT/jeep trail intersections sometimes
confusing, and stopped often to consult our maps. In the
afternoon we passed Pilot Rock, a stony pillar that we had
been able to see since the day we started. It gave us a real
sense of progress to be able to pass this milestone.

We trudged into camp at 5:30, weary and sore. Nary a
flat piece of ground was to be had, so we settled for a gently
sloping forest floor uphill from the local water source, a small
spring. The spring itself and the surrounding forest were en-
closed with fencing to keep cattle from fouling the water.
Near the spring was a ramshackle building. Collapsing and
damp, it offered no protection from the elements save as a
wind-break for our baths.

JULY 20

**Log: 14 miles, from "Fenced-In Spring" to Hyatt Reservoir. Dusty
and hot.**

Lee's journal: We bypassed some of the PCT today
and took a dirt road shortcut. Saved ourselves about
a mile and a half, and it was worth it. We met
another hiker, Jed, with his dog, at Little Hyatt who
had done the same thing—he doesn't think much of
the way the PCT has been re-routed, and says he
will take alternate routes if it saves distance or goes

past more lakes and accessible water. He is doing just the portion from Soda Springs to Fish Lake now, although he has done all of California.

Called home from the resort. Bought cinnamon rolls and a quart of milk to eat at camp, followed by a spaghetti dinner. Spirits are better but feet are just as sore. We are both showing the strain. Both of us took aspirin today to ease our sore feet. Our bodies need to get used to the loads, and our feet to the pounding. Our trail is only a few days old and the victor is uncertain—we are barely holding our own.

Ann's journal: Because we stopped two miles short of our intended camp yesterday, we added the miles onto today's distance. Stopped for lunch at Green Springs Summit and loaded up with aspirin again, which is what kept me going today. By the time we got into camp here, the aspirin had worn off, and I was about shot. Lee is stiff and sore just like me and we must make quite a sight hobbling around camp.

Did we really think this was fun? Of course not. Sore feet, sore backs, ill humor and long miles added up to nothing but unpleasantness.

We kept going because we knew our muscles *would* adapt to the heavy loads, and that our feet *would* adapt to the mile-after-mile days. We kept going because new and beautiful country appeared around every bend in the trail; because finding our way was a challenge and an adventure, and the companionship we shared was uplifting.

Underlying all this was our desire to see our project through, and not quit at the first hardship. We had no way of knowing, but things would get worse before they got better!

JULY 21

Log: 12.6 miles, from Hyatt Reservoir to Griffin Road. Hot and cloudless. Saw a scarlet tanager. Water scarce.

Lee's journal: I am still suffering from a very sore right heel; every step can be painful. I took two aspirin at lunch to help make it the last four miles to camp. It appeared Ann was going on will power alone today.

Looking ahead at the map, we probably will take several alternate routes to ease the distance by a few miles and to get to more pleasant campsites.

A hummingbird was just feeding on a columbine near me and I got a close-up view of it for several moments.

This trek is long and difficult. I am sometimes reminded of parts of *Thoughts from the Breakdown Lane*, when the runner talks of "the child" and "the adult." At times along the trail, my adult has a hard time controlling my child. I believe Ann is going through the same feelings.

Ann's journal: A few minutes left until the rice and chicken is ready. We made our scheduled twelve miles today under blistering sun. This is a dry, dusty, oven-baked land. I will be glad—I think—to get to the Sky Lakes.

The hiker Jed, whom we met yesterday, suggested taking an alternate route to Sky Lakes by way of Lake of the Woods. It used to be part of the old Oregon Skyline Trail, he said. So we have decided to take his suggestion. A regular lakeside campground, then, tomorrow night. And maybe even *ice cream* as we walk past the resort on the east side, which I have been thinking about today as I toiled under the hot sun.

About two miles from camp this afternoon, on a long ascent, we were met face-on by a couple of young boys on speeding bicycles! They appeared from nowhere and rode off into nowhere without a word. Gave us a start.

Slog, slog—on and on—until *finally* we came to the Griffin Pass Road, dropped down to it and located the little pond and campsite. I was covered with a rime of salt, my feet were on the verge of revolt, my skin was slowly broiling from the sun—and we were almost out of water. After treating a couple of quarts of water from the inlet stream, we set up camp, then—bath time! With the sun out, there was no need to hurry. The water was still icy cold, but we weren't left blue and shivering. I sat for several minutes and soaked my poor feet in the cold water.

Fixed a ripped-out seam in one of Lee's pack pockets after dinner. I brought my little gold-and-silver embroidery scissors as part of our repair kit and find it's nice to have something so familiar and civilized along with me out here.

Lee has asked me a couple of times if I think we'll "make it." Being an optimist, of course I think we'll make it—although my body doesn't agree right now!

That night Lee walked barefoot to the end of a log to get a better view of the moon—and cut open a blister on the bottom of his foot, slicing into the new skin growing underneath. We hoped it wouldn't become troublesome.

We had good views of Mount Shasta.

JULY 22

Log: 15.4 miles, from Griffin Pass Road to Aspen Point Campground
on Lake of the Woods. Hot. Water scarce.

Ann's journal: Putting on my boots this morning was an exercise in torture. Then we had trouble locating the trail at Griffin Pass, and when we found it, it led through a bog full of Oregon's finest mosquitoes. We slathered Muskol on our already-sweaty bodies and plowed on. Climbed and climbed to good views of Mount Shasta, Mount Ashland and Old Baldy.

After our high point of about 6300 feet, we made a long descent of three or four miles to the junction with the Lake of the Woods Road, which we followed in hot, dry air under afternoon sun. By this time I had developed a shin strain from trying to compensate for the pain of my feet. *This* is wilderness adventure? Actually, our long descent today was through very pretty forest, and I wished that I felt good enough to just swing right along through it.

Lee's journal: Trudging along the roadside on the way to Lake of the Woods with our heavy packs and sore feet, we watched enviously as cars sped

The tarp with mosquito netting at Lake of the Woods.

past us, covering in a few minutes the distance it would take us hours to walk. We debated the integrity of accepting a ride if one were offered, but concluded that we really wanted to walk the entire way.

Now that camp is set up, my poor feet ache! There isn't a position they are comfortable in. They have been made to walk many miles confined in dark, wet, smelly boots and now that they're free, they won't let me hear the last of it. Poor Ann, her feet are a fright too.

Ann's journal: We did stop at the resort, which was ¼-mile round-trip off our route. I was a growly bear about exerting the extra effort to go the extra ¼-mile, but went, finally, and once there gobbled popsicles and soda! Highlight of the day!

JULY 23 and 24

Log: Layover at Lake of the Woods.

We decided it was best to remain at Aspen Point Campground at Lake of the Woods for two layover days. Although the stop was unscheduled, we needed the rest to let ourselves recover. Lee's feet were improving, but mine were still blistered and sore. Having to stop for a layover was disappointing: our carefully planned schedule was now thrown awry, and we would lose the lodge reservations at Crater Lake that had been made months earlier.

Because he was feeling better, Lee found the layover a little harder to endure than I did:

Lee's journal: This layover was scheduled for Sky Lakes and fishing! At least our humor is still holding. We can still laugh at small jokes between us, and at my unconscious and hilarious malaprops.

We have been comparing the differences among the Shafer and Hartline guidebook, the National Forest Service map, and the Sky Lakes Wilderness map. Small mileage errors can be devastating if you're at the end of your endurance. We are also discovering that "on-route water" in the guidebook means *exactly* that, and that water can be fairly close "off-route," which we didn't consider when planning the trip.

After taking inventory and replanning our schedule,
I read aloud the information on the back of the
Sky Lakes map and we laughed at some of the obvious
things it said, which I guess are not so obvious to
someone who has little experience in the backcountry.
Man has certainly surrounded himself with too many
"conveniences" and I imagine most people would be
hard-pressed to survive without them.

We ate meals at the Lake of the Woods Resort, where
there was also a small store and a telephone. I called the
Klamath Falls Ranger Station for information on the Devil's
Peak area, and was told "ice axe and crampons recommended."
We had hoped to use the Puck Lakes Trail to bypass Devil's
Peak, but the Ranger's office said that trail has been abandoned
and might be difficult to follow.

We pondered that information awhile. We didn't want to
be beaten; nevertheless, it was discouraging to receive reports
of such trail conditions. Lee tried to call Don Hinton for
information on the Puck Lakes Trail but was unable to reach
him.

Lee's journal: It is easy to sit in the comforts of
this camp and talk ourselves into thinking such a
trip is impossible, of imagining things far worse
than they really are—like our first night at Wrangle
Gap. So we have decided to continue and see what
we'll find. We figure we can always turn back, call
for help, and have someone drive us to Crater Lake
if all else fails.

With nothing to do for two days, we both found ourselves
thinking of home and family. July 23rd happened to be my
daughter Amber's sixteenth birthday. I thought back to the
day she was born in a military hospital in Taiwan, and how
very different both my life and hers were now.

Lee, recently divorced, wrote: "Perhaps a layover day with
nothing to do is more than my mind can handle right now.
To have gone through the changes of the past year and to find
myself now hundreds of miles from home with nothing but a
backpack is quite strange."

About mid-afternoon of our last day at Aspen Point, we
walked down to the lake for a swim. The wind was strong,
but the water wasn't *too* cold, and we were glad to rinse dust
and dirt off.

Ann's journal: Back at camp we washed our feet as we both have to be careful to keep our various injuries clean and un-infected. Lee's cut foot looks fine.

For dinner at the resort, we were going to order the same thing we had last night, but as soon as I began to give my order to the waitress, she said, "You can't have that; it's what you had last night! You gotta try something different!"

My mouth fell open with surprise and I obediently changed my order. After Lee stopped laughing, he did the same.

The weather seems to be changing—the wind is constant and strong, blowing clouds up the lake to gather, no doubt, over our next several days' camps. The air is much cooler.

Our last night at Aspen Point was not very restful, with loud music, noisy cars, kids, and lights. We agreed that we now had a List of Places Not to Camp: (1) shelters with porcupines and (2) next to youth groups in campgrounds. The ground seemed hard as concrete. In the middle of the night, Lee gave me a shove and told me not very pleasantly to "move over!" Apparently I had edged him clear off his own foam pad, but at the time I thought his tone of voice was most uncalled-for. We were both awake before our little alarm sounded.

We were very glad to have a tiny alarm clock with us. Carrying one had been recommended to us by another hiker who had given us advice before we started the trip. We picked a battery-powered digital wrist watch with several different functions, and then removed the wrist band. We used the alarm to wake us in the morning, and the timer for processing drinking water, and for cooking.

JULY 25

Log: 12.5 miles, from Aspen Point Campground to Island Lake. Partly clear skies and cool temperatures. A couple of small snow patches.

Lee's journal: After a restless night on the rock-hard ground at Aspen Point, we awoke at 6am, and were on our way a little before 8am. Sky was grey, with some wind and rain. At the first crossing of Cascade Canal, we saw the same person with horse and donkey that we had seen previously at Grizzly Creek. Also saw a woman and child on horseback. They were

Fishing in the Sky Lakes Wilderness.

staying a week at Fourmile Lake and had ridden up to Long Lake.

Island Lake at last! The water is extremely warm and I had no success at fishing. The fish must be out in the middle where the water is deeper and cooler. We expected to have the whole place to ourselves, but after we got here a solo hiker came through; he didn't expect anyone else here, either.

Ann started out fine, but about half-way here her leg and feet began giving her problems again. She may make it to Crater Lake, but I don't think she can go much past that. We will take it easy and hope for the best.

Ann's journal: Felt good to break camp and set off, even if we did walk the first mile on road and in the rain. Up to Highway 410, then west to the Rye Spur Trail to Fourmile Lake, then into the Sky Lakes Wilderness to Island Lake, passing several other lakes on the way. We are camped at just under 6000 feet, with no snow around.

My leg began to hurt about halfway through the day—a new pain in a different muscle. The rest of me feels pretty good, though.

A tree near where we are camped has the names of several men carved into it who visited here in 1888. This is an historic spot. One of the men, Judge Waldo, was responsible for having this area set aside as part of the Forest Reserve.

The mosquitoes here are fierce and we have been plagued with them since this morning. I didn't approve of spending $4.15 on a spray can of Cutter's at Lake of the Woods Resort, but now I'm glad we have it, as our Muskol probably won't last us. Bath was a quick affair because of the vicious little devils.

JULY 26

Log: 8.4 miles, from Island Lake to Margurette Lake. Hot with strong wind, blue sky; a few snow patches on the trail.

On our way through the Sky Lakes basin we stopped to admire the many lakes that sparkled in the sun. At one point, Lee set up his fishing pole and spent an hour or so angling in Heavenly Twin Lake. We had scheduled only a few miles this day, so were able to poke along and relax. I didn't feel like fishing; my feet hurt, and I was concerned about a blister that seemed to be festering.

> *Ann's journal:* I have found a sunny—if somewhat breezy and ant-infested—place near the shore, and have taken my boots and socks off. I'm positive that these Gore-tex boots don't allow my feet to breathe as regular leather boots do. My socks are always quite damp and matted together, and my feet are always hot and sticky.
>
> This morning we soaked my painful toe, and Lee bandaged it with Second Skin, gauze and tape. It doesn't hurt at all! I had a great morning hiking along through this pretty forest with lots of little lakes, but our next two days worry me some as they both will be demanding.
>
> Lee apparently has had no luck fishing. I see him coming around the lake, on his way back.

We set up camp in mid-afternoon at Margurette Lake, on a windy promontory just off the main trail.

> *Lee's journal:* Used a large Super-duper lure and caught a rainbow about 15 inches long; beautiful fish. Couple

of casts later lost the lure—damn.

In the evening used mosquito flies and caught two eastern brook trout of about 11 and 9 inches and had several other bites.

Met two men this evening who are doing the PCT north-to-south. They were able to give us information on the Devil's Peak saddle, which they had just come over. They had no problems. Now we're in a quandary over which trail to take—the PCT or the Puck alternate: each has its advantages and questions.

Also talked with the sports editor of the Medford paper who was out for a day hike.

Ann's journal: What with fishing, socializing, and a late dinner, we're staying up late tonight. Both of us are writing by sharing the light of one candle lantern, which flickers whenever the strong wind blows around the sides of the tarp.

JULY 27

Log: 7.5 miles, from Margurette Lake to Honeymoon Creek. Little wind, moderate temperatures.

The distance from Margurette Lake to Honeymoon Creek was only a few miles, but we spent the better part of the day at it. This was the day we crossed the Devil's Peak/Lee Peak saddle. Feeling that Fate had put several obvious hints in our path, we decided to abandon the Puck Lake Trail idea, and just head right for the top of the saddle, telling ourselves that we would turn around if the snow got too dangerous to cross. I was carrying an ice axe, but Lee was not (he had wanted to save the room for his fishing gear; now it didn't seem like such a good idea!).

Ann's journal: Somehow we missed a trail junction and ended up on the old Oregon Skyline, which, unknown to us, led right to the Devil's Peak/Lee Peak saddle. The climb was steep and we were in snow. The trail disappeared. We just kept going. Before long my muscle knotted and sent shooting pains through my leg. I could hardly move the leg to take a step and wondered a time or two if I indeed would make it. In an eternity, we came out on snowfree slope, and we had marvelous views of Mount Shasta, Mount Mc Loughlin, and Klamath Lake.

Shortly after, we came to a saddle on the other
side of which was a solid basin of snow. *That* couldn't
be the way! We turned and went the opposite direction. Just where *were* we, anyway? In a quarter-
mile, Lee put down his pack. "Let's walk up to the
ridge," he said, "and see where we are." In a few
steps we were on top of the ridge, looking down
the other side into a basin of lakes. Maps and
compass came out.

Actually, there was only *one* place we could be,
but it took us some time to realize it. After we
walked up to the very summit of the ridge, it dawned
on us— we were on *top* of Devil's Peak, 7582 feet.
Nothing around us was any higher than we were.

The solid basin of snow turned out to be our
route, after all, and we wondered how we were going
to descend. Retracing the quarter-mile, we stepped
onto the snow at the saddle. I put on rain pants
and glissaded to the bottom in no time. With no
ice axe, Lee was uneasy about descending, and he
lowered his pack with a length of tarp cord, then
slowly plunge-stepped down.

Finding the trail at the bottom of the basin was
a chore. Lee dropped his pack and ranged up and
down. We couldn't see any tracks from the two
men we'd talked to yesterday.

Exhausted, with my leg aching, I stood in the sun and
rested while Lee tried to find the route. He came across a
trail that was unmarked and unsigned, but glad for any path,
we took it. At a junction in a couple of miles, it was signed
"PCT." We breathed sighs of relief.

Continuing on the PCT, we soon came to Honeymoon
Meadows and set up a comfortable camp at one end of it.
The afternoon was sunny and warm. But Lee and I were
feeling the strain of the exhausting day, and reflected the
tension in our journals:

Lee's journal: Ann and I seem to be having a problem. Perhaps I am too tired. Perhaps the strain of
"working" at the trail is keeping us distant. I wonder
if she can go on after Crater Lake or not.

Ann's journal: Hiking and camp chores are all "business" with very little time for us. I have seen a

different side of Lee recently; he has been cross and
distant.

JULY 28

Log: 20.7 miles, from Honeymoon Creek to Mazama Campground at
Crater Lake National Park. Snow over most of the trail from
Big Bunchgrass to Highway 62.

Looking back, I see this day as the low point of the
entire hike for me. As if losing the trail several times in snow,
running out of drinking water, and being tired, dirty, and
hungry were not enough, my leg still hurt, my blistered toe
was infected, and my eyes were sunburned because I hadn't
put on my sunglasses soon enough on the snow.

> *Lee's journal:* Today was a forced march of sorts.
> We hiked over twenty miles, with an energy bar
> split between us about 11am, lunch about 4:30pm,
> and dinner finally after 9 at night. Quite a day.
>
> Snow on the trail and a slow pace were problems,
> but we've made it this far. This trip is really putting
> the test to us.

With the help of a friendly ranger, we were able to phone
the lodge from the Park entrance and reserve a cabin at the
rim for the following night.

Entering the campground, we were directed to a campsite
which was "peaceful and quiet," according to the campground
manager. I'm sure he thought he was doing us a favor, but
as we walked to our assigned location, we discovered that it
was at a far corner of the campground, *another* half-mile away!

JULY 29

Log: 6 miles, from Mazama Campground to Crater Lake. Temperature
hot with a light breeze.

> *Lee's journal:* Arrived at Crater Lake early this
> afternoon. On the way, we stopped at the Post
> Office in the Park Headquarters building and picked
> up our first food box. The hike today went quickly:
> only about six miles from the campground up to
> the Crater Lake rim. It was nice to take it easy,
> knowing we had a room waiting at the other end,
> with a *shower.* People sure take such conveniences
> for granted.
>
> The transition from backwoods to civilization is
> something of a shock. One minute we're snowbound,

Reaching Crater Lake was our first big accomplishment.

hunting for a trail and hoping we're not lost, and the next minute we're with a bunch of tourists admiring a lake at a resort!

Ann's journal: From the Park Headquarters building, we took the Munson Creek shortcut up to the crater rim, saving us a couple of miles of road-walking. Coming over the edge to see the lake unfolding before us was quite a thrill.

We are staying in Cabin F, and here we are able to spread out all our things to air. We washed piles of laundry and hung them on tarp cords which Lee strung all over the little porch. I sat in the sun to let my feet dry out; they are looking much better, except for that one toe. I invested in a phone call to Dr. W to discuss my various ailments with him.

As I was strewing laundry about the porch, a rented car drove up to the adjoining cabin—we had neighbors! Since we shared the porch with that cabin, I was quick to apologize for our laundry and to explain our situation.

The man and woman were stylishly dressed and spoke with big-city accents. Although they seemed politely interested in our travels, they couldn't grasp the concept of travelling for so many weeks on foot just to reach Canada. Their comments made it apparent that they thought we were just "killing time" by doing it the "hard way."

"Well," said the woman patronizingly, "I suppose that's one of the benefits of being *unemployed*, isn't it?" I was left speechless.

We spent the afternoon unwinding and figuring out just what we were going to do. We decided that we would continue as hiking partners until one or the other of us had had enough.

That evening we had a meal at the small restaurant above the gift shops. Lee was so hungry he ordered *two* complete salad-and-sandwich dinners, and stuffed himself gloriously. I had had my heart set on ice cream at Crater Lake ever since we started, and had put off having an ice cream cone all day, so as to savor it for dessert. But by the time we finally went to the counter to get it—the fountain was closed! I was terribly disappointed. We bought cookies, but they weren't a satisfactory substitute.

We walked along the rim of the caldera.

CRATER LAKE TO OLALLIE LAKE

JULY 30

Log: 14 miles, from Crater Lake to a spot just inside the Park's north boundary. Hot and dry. Thunder clouds.

The Pacific Crest Trail has been re-routed around Crater Lake to keep it away from the distractions of civilization and traffic. In doing that, however, the trail is now in viewless forest, with none of the glorious scenery for which Crater Lake is famous.

We weren't about to spend the day in forest when we could be walking right along the edge of the great caldera, so we planned to walk the Rim Road and pick up the PCT again where it crossed the North Access Road some miles away.

In the morning we ate a genteel breakfast in the Crater Lake Lodge restaurant—in our hiking clothes—before setting out with our huge and heavy packs once more.

> *Lee's journal:* The last twenty-four hours has been a study in contrasts: the comfortable, sophisticated Lodge, the room with shower and hot water, the spectacular views around Rim Village and along the road; then, turning our backs on civilization, we descended from the cool, snowy heights into a dry, dusty, viewless desert, and wilderness once more.
>
> As we paused at the last viewpoint before leaving the rim, a little girl asked us where we were

from. "Seattle," we replied.

She wanted to know where we were going with our big packs. "Seattle," we replied again, smiling. "Why," she said with surprise, "you're walking home!"

We headed down the North Access Road, stopping at one point to melt snow for water for our camp tonight. We met a couple from the East Coast who are hiking from Mount Hood to Lake Tahoe. They had spent the night about three miles north of Highway 138, also melting snow for water.

They told us that a spot on the north side of Mount Thielsen has a steep and dangerous snow slope which they avoided by dropping to Diamond Lake— they are not carrying ice axes. Now we have something more to worry about. Seems that as soon as we get around one problem, there is another one to get in our way.

Looking ahead in the guide book, it appears we will be faced with a number of days of having lots of snow, but not much water. We'll have to look closely at the map tomorrow night to plan where and when to camp from Thielsen to Odell Lake.

We have come almost 150 miles. It is interesting to sit back every now and then and look at how far we have come over the past days. Day by day we seem to make little progress, but looking at a several-days' interval, it is satisfying to see what we have done.

We need to spend more time enjoying what we are doing and not get wrapped up in a day-to-day grind. Being a "tourist" for a little while at Crater Lake was fun. As we walked the rim this morning we took our time, took lots of pictures, and enjoyed the view and talking to people. We need to do more of that, although this next section of trail isn't exactly suited for strolling.

Maybe we will spend an extra day at the next nice resort and have some time to enjoy one another's company again. When Ann gets tired, she also gets fed up with my approach to things. I wonder how we will tackle the *next* stretch of dry, dusty trail.

Ann's journal: We turned off the North Access Road and were on the PCT again, heading off through dry, hot, dusty forest. Although we left the Lodge at

8:45 this morning, here it was 3pm, and we still had
miles to go.

I was getting tired. The mosquitoes were out in
full force and the dust was thick. We had no extra
water, as we needed all we were carrying for camp
tonight. Hot, hot, hot. This was probably one of
the worst sections we have come through.

About a mile or two from the Park boundary, we
ran across some old, hard snow patches. Snow means
water! On the spur of the moment, Lee said, "Hey,
we should camp here," and that sounded great. I
had been wondering how I would be able to sleep
tonight, all covered with dust and bug repellant, but
the snow would save us.

Lee strung up the tarp while I melted snow. We
drank. And for a bath, we scrubbed with chunks of
the rock-hard snow that we chipped off with my ice
axe!

I was pleased that—although I am pooped—my feet
and legs aren't giving me the problems they had been.
No stabbing pains, no blisters rubbing raw. Maybe
I'm finally adjusting, after a hundred-some miles.

Our camp that night was only a wide spot in the trail.
We had to clear some branches away for room to set up the
tarp, and we cooked almost in the middle of the path. Yet,
because of a patch of snow, we thought we were fortunate
indeed!

JULY 31

Log: 11.5 miles, from "Wide-Spot Camp" to Diamond Lake Resort.
Dusty, dry and hot. Malathion sprayed every Friday, according
to signs near Diamond Lake.

Lee's journal: After we crossed Highway 138, we
stopped so I could fix a sock. Then we looked at
the map and started talking about the trail ahead.
Should we avoid Thielsen by taking an alternate
route? The more we discussed it, the more we
realized we could talk ourselves into going either
way. Finally I decided that Fate had arranged for
us to meet the couple who told us about the
problem, therefore we should heed the signs and
take the bypass.

As we walked an abandoned jeep road, I thought

about stopping at the Diamond Lake Resort, getting a room, and taking a shower—it would make up for not spending two nights at Crater Lake as we originally had planned. So when we got to the Resort, that's what we did.

The "room" is actually a modern cabin the size of a small house. We enjoyed buying milk, candy, bananas and ice cream at the store, and walking the several aisles seeing all the stuff they had—the most complete store for groceries we've seen since leaving Medford.

While we were waiting for our room, a couple approached us who had seen us on the Rim Road at Crater Lake. Had we *walked* all this way? We assured them we had. The woman was awed by Ann's covering the distance, especially with the large pack—it does look quite impressive.

Another man asked me what my pack weighed and I said about sixty pounds. He looked at Ann's pack and—tongue in cheek—she said hers weighed sixty-*five* pounds! He said it was probably from me walking behind her and adding things from my pack to hers!

Ann called home to get another ice axe mailed to Shelter Cove, our next supply stop. We are getting tired of worrying about crossing snow because I don't have one.

Ann's journal: Reading over what I have written lately, I realized I have condensed some very busy days into a few paragraphs. I hope that what I've put down here will still bring back the memories when this trip is done.

After a brisk swim in Diamond Lake, we had dinner in the Resort's family dining room. The meal was delicious, but even hungry as I was, I couldn't finish it all. Lean already from years of distance running, Lee was feeling the effects of not enough food, and he had no trouble finishing both my dinner and his!

AUGUST 1

Log: 15.7 miles, from Diamond Lake Resort to Maidu Lake. Hot with threatening clouds; light wind.

From Diamond Lake, at about 5200 feet, we now had to

The rugged north face of Mount Thielsen.

climb back up to the PCT, which had been waiting for us two
thousand feet above in the snow. On our way up the Tipsoo
Trail to intersect the PCT, we could look back to the north
side of Mount Thielsen which we had avoided. It was steep
and snowy.

Even before we reached the PCT again, we were hiking in
snow that made route-finding difficult and slowed our pace.
Although marked with metal "blazes" on trees and posts,
the PCT is not sufficiently marked for easy travelling on snow.

> *Ann's journal:* Today was almost 16 miles' worth,
> which seems like the mileage we're *supposed* to be
> doing. It felt good to be hiking today, although
> after all that snow and searching for the trail, I
> was sure ready to stop walking. It seems as though
> Lee can go on forever: he just strides right over logs,

We searched for signs of the trail on snow-covered slopes.

he never takes a misstep, he never gets tired. I just watch in envy. He could make better time alone.

The high point of the Pacific Crest Trail in Oregon is located on the shoulder of Tipsoo Peak in the snow at 7560 feet. We had lunch huddled on the lee side of a log near that high point, and at a trail junction a few miles farther, followed an alternate route on the Oregon Skyline Trail that would take us past several lakes, and keep us from struggling with the deep snows on the re-routed PCT over Diamond Peak, not too far ahead.

Lee's journal: Maidu Lake is almost a mile off our main trail, but the closest source of water at this point. Tried fishing and caught a couple of six-inchers on a mosquito fly. If I worked at it I could probably catch quite a few, but after walking almost 16 miles—most of it on snow and hunting for the trail—I didn't feel like battling wits with a trout.

Ann's journal: The mosquitoes here are fierce, and they slip into the tarp at every opportunity. We can't kill them all.

A heron came by the lake at dusk and Lee had quite a conversation with it.

AUGUST 2

Mosquitoes at Maidu Lake were just as bad in the morning
as they had been the evening before, even though a heavy dew
had fallen and the air was very chilly. The inside of the tarp
was covered with water droplets that splatted down on us as
we brushed against our ceiling. We ate breakfast inside the
tarp to escape being eaten ourselves, then hurried through our
packing to get away from the mosquitoes and into hiking to
warm ourselves.

Ann's journal: Again today it felt good to be out
on the trail. We hiked seven miles to Tolo Camp
without a break, then stopped to share one of Lee's
energy bars—chocolate and peanut butter!

From Tolo Camp we went another six miles to
Windigo Pass before stopping for lunch.

Lee's journal: At a road crossing today two men
drove by and stopped to ask us for directions. We
told them we didn't know; we had only stopped
for lunch on our way to Canada!

Ann's journal: We ended up at Nip and Tuck Lakes
about 4pm. Lots of our things were still wet from
this morning, so we strung a line to dry them out.

The lakes are shallow, only knee-deep, and the
water is warm as a bathtub. The sun was out, no
mosquitoes were around, and I sat in the sun to
air-dry.

Lee's journal: No fish in the lakes, but lots of leeches.
The warm lake water was very pleasant.

I'm tired—and also hungry. Meals don't seem to
be enough any more. I could easily eat *both* our
helpings. This could get to be a problem. My
thoughts today were on tacos and fresh-baked salmon.
Got to quit thinking about food.

We keep expecting to meet other PCT hikers, but
we don't. I wonder where they all are.

I could walk faster and cover a few more miles
by myself, but I do enjoy Ann's company. In com-
parison to two weeks ago, we have improved greatly
in covering distance. We need to improve still more
to make this trip really comfortable.

Water quality at lakes such as Nip and Tuck was very questionable. The water was virtually stagnant, but it was all we had. As usual, we treated drinking water with our iodine solution, and boiled our cooking water. When possible, we collected water from inlet streams—no guarantee of purity, but better perhaps than from the lake shore.

We felt that bathing with soap in any lake was inexcusable pollution. Our dips in lakes and rivers were for recreation only. To wash, we filled our plastic gallon water jug and carried it well away from the water source. Then, one person would wash while the other poured—a whole "bath" with a gallon of water! The dirty water would sink into the ground and filter impurities before reaching the lake again.

AUGUST 3

Log: 14 miles, from Nip and Tuck Lakes to Diamond View Lake. Temperature hot. Water easily available from lakes and streams.

In the morning we had pancakes for breakfast, truly a luxury meal because of the time required to cook and clean up afterward. We thought the pancakes were great—hot, filling, and sweet. We sprinkled granulated sugar on them and ate them with our fingers.

Cooking at ground level is not the most convenient arrangement, and this morning Lee's boot and the bowl of pancake batter collided. The bowl tipped over on top of his boot—what a mess! (Luckily we didn't lose all the batter.)

There he sat, trying to keep the pancake in the pan from scorching with one hand, and trying to save the remainder of the batter with the other. It was a hilarious scene, but since Lee was spouting expletives I tried to stifle my laughter.

When he finally managed a smile and said, "Do you want a picture?" I ran to get my camera. After taking the photo, I finished cooking the pancakes while he mopped up his boot.

Two miles after leaving Nip and Tuck Lakes, we stopped at deep, cold Oldenburg Lake for Lee to try fishing. The shore of the lake was brushy and forested, and a wind was blowing—two reasons for me *not* to try fishing! I busied myself with other things, and watched Lee fish his way around to the end of the lake. He caught his hook on the bottom, and waded out to retrieve it. "Very refreshing!" he called to me, as he stood in icy water three feet deep.

Oldenburg Lake had an almost spooky feeling to it. Many downed trees were strewn around the campsites. Not another soul was there, but we found several things—a riding quirt, a towel, and a very nice western jacket, in obvious places, as though people had left in a hurry.

> *Lee's journal:* Decided to keep the jacket since it fits Ann, and would be a shame to have it go to waste. Unfortunate part is that it weighs a lot; tomorrow will be Ann's turn to carry it.
>
> About half a mile in on the Whitefish Trail we met another PCT hiker named Curt who had started in Canada. He had left Odell Lake that morning and was in a hurry to get to Crater Lake because his friends at home had forgotten to mail his supply box to Odell Lake! He was taking this alternate route since it is a few miles shorter than going over Diamond Peak.
>
> He told us there were several other PCTers on the trail ahead of us by a few days, and also that we would be encountering snow in the Three Sisters Wilderness. He had been hiking with a dog, but it was hurt by a porcupine in Washington and he had taken it to friends in Yakima. After getting to Seiad Valley, he planned to come back and pick up the dog, then, being short on money, work the eastern Washington apple harvest.

We visited with Curt as we were eating our lunch. It never failed that while we were sitting there in the dust with our boots and socks off, some hiker would come around the bend. I began to wonder how come *we* never came upon other hikers sitting by the trail with *their* boots and socks off—were we the only ones who took such complete rest breaks?

> *Lee's journal:* Diamond View Lake is shallow and warm—no fish and apparently no leeches. It felt good to take a bath after getting here.
>
> I hope there is a resort at Odell Lake with a good restaurant, or at least a store where I can get lots of food! Curt told us there was a shower for hikers and a place to do washing, and that Trapper Creek Campground is free for the first night for PCT hikers.
>
> Looking from here over to Diamond Peak shows us how much snow is there and what we would have faced going that way; it's a good thing we took

the alternate route. I wonder if I will be able to
keep this up. My feet are sore after about ten miles.
My shoulder starts to hurt after a few miles. Seems
I spend most of the day shifting my pack around to
help my shoulder, or walking carefully to help my
feet.

Perhaps we're carrying too much. We could cut
weight by not carrying fishing or photography equipment.

I am eager to get to Odell Lake, get our next
supply box, and head into different country. A lot
of what we've been through seems to have been
just putting in time, with only a couple of high spots
(Sky Lakes and Crater Lake). I hope the next
section will contain a lot of scenic and interesting
places instead of a high point only once in a while.

Ann's journal: We've been out two and a half weeks
now, and with a layover day at Odell Lake tomorrow
will be four days behind schedule, with little chance
of making up the time. At Odell Lake we'll get
our next supply box, with eleven days' worth of
food. Our packs will be heavier for this next section
than they were when we began!

This was, overall, a very pleasant day, with easy
trail, reasonable distances between water, and nice
weather except when the wind died down and the
mosquitoes came up. Our camp at Diamond View
is quite comfortable. Although the mosquitoes are
fierce, we are relatively safe in the tarp.

I feel good about the day, the hiking, and my
choice of companion. Lee is no longer so disagree-
able. Has his attitude changed? Perhaps *my* attitude
has changed, too. I no longer come into camp at
the end of the day tired and hurting, and that certainly affects my mood.

AUGUST 4 and 5

Log: 5.2 miles, from Diamond View Lake to Shelter Cove Resort on
Odell Lake. Blue skies, light wind. Layover day at Shelter Cove.

Setting off from Diamond View Lake at 6:30am, we
quickly hiked an easy five miles down Trapper Creek to
Shelter Cove Resort. The morning was pretty and cold, with

the pink light of dawn glistening on the snows of Diamond
Peak. Striding up to the little General Store at the resort, we
parked our packs on the porch and clumped inside.

A small sandwich counter took up one side of the room,
and a few aisles of groceries and fishing tackle the other. At
the back, we found the "Post Office"—a small cabinet hung
on the wall, with hikers' boxes stacked on the floor underneath
it. We were happy to see that our supply boxes as well as
Lee's ice axe had arrived safely.

Instead of camping at the local campground, Lee wanted
to stay in one of the resort cabins. It was very nice to have
a real roof, but it made the transition back to hiking all the
more difficult. Staying in the cabin was also very expensive,
as we stayed two nights there, and paid resort-prices for
groceries.

We spent the day of our arrival cleaning out our packs,
washing laundry in a real washing machine, washing ourselves
with hot water, writing postcards, eating, and sleeping.

> *Lee's journal:* It looks like part of this rustic resort
> was destroyed at one time and the new owners
> are trying to salvage what is left. The fishing looks
> good; some large brown trout are taken out of the
> lake.

The general store at Shelter Cove Resort.

Ann's journal: The Stroms, who run the resort, have
been here for two summers. It's an awful lot of
work; they seem *always* busy. The resort appears
a bit in need of care, but they are upgrading it
little by little. Our cabin shows signs of fresh paint,
and the work they are doing on the store is an
improvement.

Lee's journal: The only problem with resort-stopping
is it costs quite a bit of money. We'll have to watch
it if we're going to have enough.

I find I am getting tired of doing "hiking things"
all the time. Packing, repacking, washing clothes,
greasing boots—I would like some other diversion,
like a movie or a novel. We did spend a little time
rowing on the lake; however, one oarlock wasn't
very good so we couldn't go far, but we appreciated
being able to propel ourselves in another way besides
our feet!

Ann's journal: Food! We had a huge pancake breakfast, and we have also done in (that is, Lee has
mostly done in) a dozen eggs, a pint of cottage cheese,
a can of pears, a package of cheese, a couple of
tomatoes, two cans of orange juice, two cans of
peas, a can of chicken and half a box of rice.

All to myself I had a jar of peanut butter. Oh
yes, and add to that list two dozen tortillas, some
doughnuts, and for Lee *four* cans of beer *and* a
bottle of wine!

Lee is antsy at having nothing to do, even though
his heels are bothering him, and he has picked out
a Reader's Digest from the "library" at the store.

AUGUST 6

**Log: 12 miles, from Shelter Cove Resort to Bobby Lake. Hot, no
wind, blue skies all day, but clouds in evening.**

We hauled our packs out of the cabin like a couple of
furniture movers, but we managed to get them on and start
hiking again. Lee said his pack was one of the heaviest he'd
ever carried—he had taken some of the food that I was
supposed to be packing, and he also had an ice axe to tote
now, as well. Our next supply point was 150 miles away.

Lee's journal: Although we both reacted fairly well

Fishing at Bobby Lake.

to our loads, we were both glad to reach camp at Bobby Lake tonight. My feet and back hurt somewhat, but the load will diminish in the days to come as we eat the food. I feel rested now after the Odell layover and I would like to get some miles in. This section is important since it takes us through probably the last snow in Oregon, and it also will put us over half-way through the state. I am looking forward to reaching Washington.

I am also looking forward to having the mosquitoes end. Unfortunately we must put up with several weeks of biting flies before we are done with insects. Maybe by September we can string the tarp without using the mosquito netting.

Tried fishing at Lower Rosary Lake without success—the fish are there but I tried for only half an hour. Had I worked at it all day I'm sure I could have caught some. Middle Rosary also looked like good fishing. I tried Bobby Lake, too. I think it is the wrong season—the water is covered with floating bugs but only a few little fish are jumping. In September this might be a good lake.

Several lakes are coming up in the next few

days and perhaps I can have better luck. It is
frustrating to carry fishing gear and not be able to
catch fish! In a way, long-distance hiking doesn't
allow much time for fishing unless you take a layover day. I haven't yet seen a spot at which I'd like
to spend a day out of our schedule; the fishing is
too unpredictable. I would rather spend the extra
day at a resort where we can relax in some comfort,
get cleaned up, and get *food*.

Hitting the trail again is bittersweet. It is hard
to leave comforts to struggle with a pack, a difficult
trail and mosquitoes for six or eight hours, but it
is gratifying to see new country, to see the progress
we've made, and to have the satisfaction of setting
up camp at the end of another day.

Ann and I seem to be doing all right with the
difficult period of Crater Lake behind us. We do
hike well together.

In the night, a thunderstorm woke us and spattered a few
rain drops on the tarp. Lee was concerned that it would
really pour on us and got up to fuss with the tarp and to
make sure our things would stay dry. I was too sleepy to
worry much about it. Although we heard several rolls of
thunder and saw lightning, the rain never got serious.

AUGUST 7

Log: 13.5 miles, from Bobby Lake to upper end of Irish Lake. Hot
and steamy southeast wind.

Lee's journal: Our trail was in woods most of the
day, except for one spot where we were able to
look south as far as Mount Thielsen. I enjoy seeing
how far we've come. Besides the viewpoint, the
only other highlights of the day were reaching
Charlton Lake and reaching Irish Lake, the northwest corner of which is our camp tonight.

Ann's journal: Leaving camp about 8am, we began
to climb, and climb, and climb. In several miles,
at a viewpoint, we finally stopped and looked at
the map—we had climbed to 6600 feet! The guidebook had neglected to mention that, and we had
neglected to study the maps closely. Got a good
view, though. The rest of the trail was through

dense forest filled with annoying mosquitoes. This
was an awfully long day for only 13.5 miles.

I drank an entire quart of water while we were
setting up camp. It's been terribly hot and muggy
today.

Lee's journal: We have several problems coming up:
some 18-mile days with no water at the ends unless
we want to go cross-country to find lakes; some
plowing through 8-foot snowdrifts that another hiker
told us about; and a glacial stream that must be
forded before 11am or the snowmelt makes it too
dangerous to cross.

We'll have to deal with these things in a couple
of days. Always problems to face. We'll study
the maps and book to try to find a way around
them. We have a limited food supply and there will
be no resorts to fall back on. Maybe we'll run into
a southbound hiker who can give us information.

Ann's journal: During our conversation between
bath and dinner, I mentioned that sometimes tromp-
ing along the trail I felt I was *too old* to be doing
something like this. To my surprise, Lee said he
sometimes felt the same way. This journey is not
a lark, but it *is* an accomplishment that we can be
proud of.

Lee's journal: Neither of us likes sore feet, bugs,
and miles and miles of sceneless walking. We both
like the feeling of accomplishment and the pretty
things we see. But I do miss my kids and the
comforts of life. Perhaps I will turn into a car-
camper after this.

AUGUST 8

Log: 16.2 miles, from Irish Lake to Dumbbell Lake. Hot; no wind.

After some rain in the middle of the night, the skies
cleared and we set out before 8am for an anticipated camp
at Cliff Lake. We both felt pretty good today, and enjoyed
(except for the mosquitoes) stopping at the several lakes we
passed.

Lee's journal: I tried fishing at Stormy Lake without
success, although I saw several good-sized fish jump.

Had lunch at Mac Lake and tried fishing with no success; didn't even see any rising.

Ann's journal: The mosquitoes pounced on us first thing this morning and got to be the *worst* we have experienced so far. They were in my hair, in my ears, all over my arms where I sweat the repellant off. I inhaled several, and by the time we got to Stormy Lake I was past my tolerance for the nasty things. I pulled my head net out of my pack—ah, relief! Not only did it keep them out of my face and hair, but also off my neck and chest. The rest I could handle. The net restricts my vision some, but is the lesser of two evils at this point.

The net brings relief.

After a few more miles we encountered a bit of breeze and the mosquitoes weren't so bad, so I just lifted the net over my head and let it fall across my shoulders. Worth its weight in gold today.

We picked up the trail of what we thought was a very sloppy PCT hiker—first he scattered corn nuts, sunflower seeds and M&Ms, then he discarded a partially empty box of Ritz crackers, then pistachio husks, all interspersed with toilet paper and wrappings from various edibles. Since we were able to see several different tracks, we decided we were following a whole group, not just one hiker. And every so often in the trail would be an arrow or sign made of sticks and pebbles.

A sign made of sticks.

Lee's journal: As we approached Cliff Lake, we heard voices. The arrows we had seen continued down the

spur trail to the lake, and so did we. At the shore
we found a group of about twelve boys all shouting,
splashing in the water and shooting slingshots. They
had taken over the shelter and the surrounding
campsites.

We could have camped on a cliff above the lake,
a nice spot; however, the noise would have spoiled
the camp for us. So with disappointment, we put
on our packs and headed for Dumbbell Lake. The
only consolation is that perhaps whatever Fate is
guiding us meant for us not to camp there. Who
knows?

Ann's journal: When we could see Dumbbell Lake
through the trees, we cut over to it to look for a
camp. Lee talked with two men who were setting
up a tent on a peninsula that juts out into the
water. We found ourselves a dandy campsite,
almost on a peninsula, too. On one side was our
private bath; on the other, space for Lee to fish.
Probably a much nicer camp than Cliff Lake, anyway.

We had our camp chores done and dinner almost
cooked when one of our neighbors came over for
a visit. He brought us a bag of raisins ("from California," he said) as a gift and sat down for a talk.

Lee's journal: We talked of our trip and his. He
and his grown son are on a three-day hike through
Mink Lake Basin. He had worked on the Crater
Lake Rim Road in the 30s, and spent a number of
years in Alaska. His son is probably about my age
and from San Jose. He doesn't really look the
hiking type. The older gentleman reminded me of
my dad several years ago, with the "older generation"
ways about him. Quite an enjoyable conversation,
even if it did delay our dinner by an hour!

Ann's journal: After our guests went home, we
turned to our neglected dinner. I figured we'd have
to put it on the stove again as it would surely be
stone cold. But it was just the right temperature,
and we gobbled it down, topping it off with tea
and pudding—and raisins—for dessert.

South Sister towers above Wikiup Plain.

AUGUST 9

Log: 17.1 miles, from Dumbbell Lake to North Fork Mesa Creek. Hot! Occasional clouds; mostly clear.

Lee's journal: We planned on a long day—17 miles— and fortunately we were able to do it, reaching Mesa Creek about 5pm. The views of South Sister, the Rock Mesa and lava flows have been very impressive, taking our minds off sore feet and bodies as we hiked the last five miles to camp.

Ann's journal: I started right out today with my headnet across my shoulders, and used it several times as the day got mosquitoe-y.

We had decided to take the PCT right over Koosah Mountain—about 6400 feet—because the guidebook praises the views so, even though the alternate Oregon Skyline Trail is 2½ miles shorter through this section and passes lakes. Climb, climb, climb—what a hot, dusty slog that was. It went on forever. A few views, yes; but then we dropped right back into forest (and clouds of mosquitoes) again. Both of us hot and tired and we grumbled some.

In a couple of more miles we dropped to Sisters Mirror Lake and had lunch, a very satisfying stop.

A mile or two after Sisters Mirror we suddenly broke out onto a spectacular scene: the PCT crosses Wikiup Plain, with South Sister towering above it on the right, all red-cinder-topped and splashed with snow fields. The Plain stretches for a couple of miles along the west side of the volcano, and is bordered by a high lava flow that solidified in mid-stream, so to speak. It was an impressive bit of trail to hike.

At the other end of the Plain we entered forest, and it was as though we crossed into a different world—green meadows, blooming flowers, tumbling creeks. We shortly came to the North Fork Mesa and picked a hasty camp. It was full of rocks, which I tossed out of the way, and old horse manure, which I did not.

Lee's journal: We are camped on the edge of the meadow in a small level spot. We were too tired to notice the established campsites farther back in the woods. This is a beautiful place. Too bad the mosquito netting needs to be up, as the whole meadow is open to the sky, surrounded by a for-ested ridge with South Sister in the distance.

Another hiker is camped east of us in a clump of trees five or six hundred feet away. He is carrying a flannel sleeping bag with just a plastic sheet for a ground cloth, and using an old-style packboard. He told us he had come in from Devil's Lake and is out for just a couple of days.

Looking over the miles coming up, we don't have any easy days scheduled unless we want to add an extra day. We've put in some long miles the past couple of days, and we really should do about 15 miles tomorrow. I am very sleepy tonight, and my heels ache. Ann appears to be quite tired.

Ann's journal: Lee said I was somewhat "touchy" this evening, so maybe I am tireder than I realize. I guess I am dwelling on some teasing remarks he made today.

With the little creek rushing by and the stars shining

brightly, we slept soundly, anticipating another beautiful day.
But about 6:30am, fog rolled in to fill our meadow, and we
packed up in a damp gloom.

AUGUST 10

Log: 16.8 miles, from North Fork Mesa Creek to South Mathieu Lake.

The fog lifted briefly in mid-morning, then settled in for
the rest of the day. Even so, we thought that the Three
Sisters Wilderness was one of the most beautiful areas—no, *the*
most beautiful—in Oregon. It was a spot to which we wanted
to return, maybe to climb South Sister, certainly to hike all
the side trails we had to pass by.

Ann's journal: Counted thirty-nine hikers on the
trail today—almost a culture shock for us. Some
were friendly and stopped to talk, others in a hurry
just said "hi." No other PCT distance hikers.

Lee's journal: The fog got thicker as we pressed
north, adding an eerie overtone to the lava flows
we passed. Fortunately we were around North
Sister by the time our views were blocked, so we
had already seen a lot.

At Minnie Scott Spring the fog lifted just enough
to give us a final spectacular view, then settled in
with much wind.

Ann's journal: We had snow to cross and lava beds
and creeks and it was quite a day. The lava fields
are most catastrophic—like someone just plopped down
blobs of goo that hardened.

Minnie Scott Spring was bubbling right out of the
ground with clear, cold water that I drank "straight."
Lee filled his canteen and then popped in an iodine
tablet before he drank, not taking *any* chances.

Lee's journal: We debated camping at Minnie Scott
Spring, but wind, fog and cold told us to keep
moving. We ended up at South Mathieu Lake which
is right on a pass. The wind is blowing strongly—the
worst wind I've ever had the tarp set up in. We
arranged camp as best we could. I fear the tarp will
be damaged in this high wind.

Using trees for a wind break, I still took my daily
shower to get the sweat and grime off. Ann settled
for a wipedown with a wet bandana.

What a night it was! The wind blew very hard until
after midnight. We stayed warm wrapped snug as mummies
in our sleeping bags with the bivvy bags over them. About
midnight Lee said, "Are you awake?" and we talked for a
few minutes. I slept soundly after that, although Lee reported that he had spent a fitful night. We were grateful that
the tarp had held.

AUGUST 11

Log: 11.5 miles, from South Mathieu Lake to Washington Ponds.
Moderate temperature; strong winds.

In the morning, although the sky was blue, the wind was
just as strong as it had been the evening before. Our gear was
as wet as if it had been rained on. We cooked and ate breakfast under the shelter of the tarp, away from the wind, then
packed quickly with numb fingers and set off. What a relief
to be heading away from that horrible camp.

Our list of Places Not To Camp now included windy
passes, as well as shelters with porcupines and camps next to
youth groups.

The access to lower Mathieu Lake, just another mile or
so farther, and with much safer and more protected camps,
has been blocked off to prevent overuse.

Mount Washington appears through the clouds.

Observatory at Mc Kenzie Pass, watching the clouds
blow around and reveal the mountains behind them.
Also important there was the garbage can—I got rid
of the several days' worth of garbage I'd been
hauling around!

Leaving the Observatory, we climbed up through
more lava again, past Belknap and Little Belknap
Craters. We met another PCT hiker going north-to-
south; he talked very casually about snow and
stream crossings, our bugaboos on the trail ahead.

This was one of the stretches about which we had been
concerned some time back ("several problems coming up," Lee
had written at Irish Lake). Water in these parts was scarce, and
springs could not always be relied upon. Where would we
camp tonight? The guidebook said that Washington Ponds were
off-trail, hard to find, and appealing only to "desperate hikers."

Lee's journal: We decided to camp at Washington
Ponds because we got conflicting reports of the
condition of Coldwater Spring: a southbound PCT
hiker said there was about 6 inches of water in the
pipe; however a group of young people said it was
dry. Since we knew horses were ahead of us (horses

drink a lot of water) and since we didn't want a difficult camp, we chose this spot.

Ann's journal: With the map and a couple of false starts, we located the lower pond without too much difficulty. It is a pretty spot. Lee strung a line and we filled it with out wet gear from the night before. Luckily it was sunny and warm with only a light breeze blowing.

Lee seemed quite tired. By the time we had camp set up, baths done, and dinner started, he was getting chilled. He ate dinner in bed, and then got up to warm his feet at the little fire I'd started.

Lower Washington Pond was really only a tarn. It probably had been sitting there stagnant since the snows melted. The water was full of gook. I cut a square of material out of the bottom of my head-net, and we used it to strain the mosquitoes, larvae, dead flies, silt, and leaves from our water supply.

Lee's journal: As we were getting ready for bed, I found a trail which we took to the upper pond, and then, on the spur of the moment, we continued beyond to open meadows almost at the base of Mount Washington. We watched the sun set on the

Lava beds near Little Belknap Crater.

hills to the south and west, and the red sunlight on Mount Washington was spectacular. It really made this "desperate" camp worthwhile.

Ann's journal: Finding our way back to camp after sunset was not so much fun. We had left camp in daylight, but now we couldn't pick out our route through the trees and I was afraid we would miss the ponds. I don't know how Lee felt, but I really had to lecture myself to control the panic. Relief set in when I saw the upper pond through the trees. Our camp was easy to find from there.

Lee's journal: I am anxious to get to Olallie and, I hope, some *food.* I need more to eat than what I am getting now; I am running too near empty.

We'll have to add some mileage onto the next days—only 11.5 miles today—but after all our problems last night it was good to have an easy camp. I shaved, we dried things, we bathed and had a fire, and took an after-dinner walk. All very nice.

AUGUST 12

Log: 13.9 miles, from Washington Ponds to Summit Lake. Hot, with strong east wind and blue sky.

Ann's journal: We went right around the corner of Mount Washington this morning and got tremendous views of all the surrounding country, including clear back to Diamond Peak.

Sunset below Mount Washington leaves us in the dark.

Lee's journal: Hiking today had some good points and some bad. The last few miles before reaching Santiam Pass were *boring!* Although we did have good views of Mount Washington and Three-Fingered Jack, they couldn't help the slogging of the miles through burned-over forest.

It was definitely a psychological plus to cross the highway (a busy one) and get into a new area.

Here was another spot with no convenient water or place to camp. Again, we headed for a "desperate" camp, leaving the PCT to go cross-country to Summit Lake on the south side of Three-Fingered Jack.

Ann's journal: We are the only ones here, although the camps look well-used. I finally managed to get some clothes washed, including my horrid, smelly old shirt, which I think is going to rot clean away before this hike is through.

Lee's journal: It is good of Ann to do laundry for both of us. She realizes I am getting low on energy. We are both getting tired and a little cranky. Fortunately, we realize what's happening and are trying our best to not let it affect us.

Ann's journal: Lee says he is *hungry!* He has lost several pounds, but he doesn't have any extra to lose. I have lost a few pounds also, but I have plenty to spare. I am holding back some on how much I eat to give him a little more.

AUGUST 13

Log: 18.5 miles, from Summit Lake to Hank's Lake. Hot, with wind blowing storm clouds up from the southwest.

Ann's journal: This morning we walked through open meadows around the side of Three-Fingered Jack, with glorious views south, west, and finally north to Mount Jefferson. We used our ice axes to cross a few snow patches. Although the snow was hard and slick, the slopes were not dangerously steep.

On the north side of Three-Fingered Jack we stopped at a pass, dropped the packs, and made an ascent of Porcupine Peak. It was good to be able to walk around without the pack on. Although it is not too heavy now, it still makes my back and

shoulders ache by mid-morning and I spend
the rest of the day continually easing the weight
from one shoulder to the other.

Lee's journal: Eighteen-and-a-half miles makes for a
long day and sore feet. In the afternoon we could
see clouds moving in from the southwest and noticed
that the wind picked up.

Ann's journal: To escape a high and exposed camp
on the PCT, we followed an abandoned route down
a gully to this camp and got things set up and baths
done just as the rain started.

Lee's journal: The timing worked out very well. It
was nice not having to set up camp in the rain.

I went fishing and got strikes on every cast, catching mostly 6"-10" brook trout. It was too late to
cook fish, so I released them all.

I am quite hungry. I believe Ann is letting me
eat more than my share to help me.

We met a couple today who had started on the
PCT near Mount Hood. They had no plan and didn't
know how far they were going. Whenever they ran
out of food, they would hitchhike to a town to buy
more. They told us the cafeteria at Timberline
Lodge has good hamburgers.

We also got information from several groups today
about the crossing of glacier-fed Russell Creek, our
next question mark. It doesn't sound like it will be
too difficult, but we're planning on an early start
tomorrow anyway.

AUGUST 14

Log: 11.9 miles, from Hank's Lake to South Fork Breitenbush River
in Jefferson Park. Hot, with wind from southwest.

Lee's journal: We set out at 6:30am for Russell
Creek, ten miles away. In the back of my mind was
concern about crossing it before the glacial melt
made it too deep and dangerous, as the guidebook
warns. I wondered what we would do if we couldn't
cross it.

Ann's journal: We dropped many hundreds of feet
from Hank's Lake to Pamelia Lake. All the creeklets

Beautiful views south from Three-Fingered Jack.

along the way were a delight, as it has been awhile since we have seen water so plentiful and run so freely.

At Pamelia Lake, our junction took us *up*—of course—the many hundreds of feet we had spent the early morning losing. As Lee says, with resignation, "Why not?" Our first creek was Milk Creek, which we rock-hopped over. Then Jeff Creek, which must have been a trickle because we didn't notice it.

Lee's journal: We pushed toward the next creek, thinking it to be Jeff Creek and still anxious about Russell. We took our boots off and waded across, and as I was waiting for Ann to put her boots back on, I looked over the map and the route description and discovered we had just forded Russell Creek! It really wasn't that bad—water just above the ankles, fast moving, and *cold*, but with a good bottom. I have forded much worse places in the Olympics.

It seems at times the book goes a little overboard. "Illegal camps" for sites within 100 feet of a lake; "desperate" for out-of-the-way water or camps; "putrid puddle" for nice-looking Pamelia Lake; "beautiful Rockpile Lake" for what looked like an ordinary

South from Park Ridge to Mount Jefferson.

shallow lake; "stagnant pond" or "unclear water" for what look like nice places. Oh well. The book has been a great help, and this trip would be difficult without the guidance it offers. Besides it does add some entertainment, and it does provide information and history of the regions we pass through.

After crossing the creek, we had no real destination in mind. Looking ahead, we found we had a thousand-foot elevation gain after we left Jefferson Park. Ann really didn't want to do that today, so we camped at the north end of the Park next to a creek.

Ann's journal: Strangely, I have felt really crummy most of the day. How can I feel this way now when I have felt so good the last few days? Lack of sleep, maybe, or good food. The heat. Something.

Lee would have liked to have gone on another five miles, just to get us closer to Olallie for tomorrow, but I didn't feel like going on.

Lee's journal: We stopped hiking about 1:30pm. It turned into a long, idle afternoon for me: it seems like we should be hiking if it is still afternoon. However, the rest probably did us some good.

Sitting around this afternoon and thinking ahead, it seems like a long way yet to go. I'm not really looking forward to the Mount Hood section or southern Washington; afraid it will be day after day of just putting the miles in. We have been spoiled by the views we've had recently. We need to just keep chinking away at the distance and we'll get there—we've already come 340 miles! Hardly seems possible.

Ann's journal: After camp was set up, I crawled into the tarp and fell asleep. When I woke up, I got my camera and went for a walk, stopping to look at flowers, and to take several photos. Jefferson Park is a huge expanse of meadows and lakes.

AUGUST 15

Log: 12.2 miles, from Jefferson Park to Olallie Lake Resort. Blue skies, no wind, and <u>hot</u>.

Early the next morning we set off to climb the 7010-foot ridge just north of Jefferson Park. The slopes of that ridge still held snow, and in the early morning they were icy, steep and dangerous. We were thankful for the ice axes. From the

North from Park Ridge to Mount Hood.

top of the ridge we could see north to Hood, Adams, and Saint Helens—we felt as though we were almost home!

As we were about to head down the north side of the ridge, two PCTers, "Rand and Jim," came over the snow from the north. We exchanged trail information with them.

> *Lee's journal:* They told us that Olallie Lake Resort has no phone, no plumbing, no electricity—and no ice cream! Ann was disappointed.
>
> We crossed quite a bit of snow. It seemed to take forever to get the miles in today.
>
> *Ann's journal:* We walked up to the little Guard Station at Olallie about 2:30 in the afternoon. As we set our packs down, one of the backcountry rangers came around the corner and said, "Your name wouldn't be Ann, would it?" I allowed as how it was and she said they'd been expecting us— we had more mail waiting for us than they'd had all summer!
>
> We collected our boxes and envelopes, and sorted things out on the picnic table behind the Guard Station. Even without showers and hot water, Lee had decided he wanted to rent a cabin here, so for twenty bucks we got four walls and a roof, a real bed, a real table, and real chairs with backs.

We sorted things out on the picnic table.

Lee's journal: We shopped at the resort and spent $25 on groceries: beer, wine, chips, cheese, eggs, margarine, bread, candy, peaches. Dinner was wine for me, root beer for Ann, chili, cheese, and bread.

Before dinner, we went to Head Lake, the local "bath house," for a swim. By the time we were done with dinner it was 9pm.

Lee had had problems with a sore toe, and in the middle of the night he awoke with it hurting. Then and there he decided to get up and soak it in warm water. He fired up our backpacking stove, put the water on, and then decided to go to the bathroom, which was an outhouse up the road. He woke me up to ask if I would watch the water. *Good grief,* I thought, half asleep.

But once I got up I remembered my candy bar that I hadn't eaten after dinner. For a 2am snack it was very good, and gave Lee a fit of laughter when he got back and found I'd eaten it all in the middle of the night.

OLALLIE LAKE TO WHITE PASS

AUGUST 16

Log: 10.3 miles, from Olallie Lake Resort to Trapper Spring. Hot with
no wind and blue sky.

As we were packing to set out in the morning, I noticed
that my brand-new boots were coming apart! I hoped they
would hold together until we reached the Columbia River and
I could have them either repaired or replaced.

Even though we had stayed overnight at Olallie Lake, we
hadn't taken a "layover"—a day without hiking—since Shelter
Cove. This fact was beginning to work away at Lee, and he
would begin to keep track of the days we had hiked without
a break.

> *Lee's journal:* Counting today we have hiked eleven
> straight days and that is too much.
>
> Originally we had scheduled a 20-mile day today,
> but we re-did the schedule to allow us some free
> time this morning, so hiked only 10 miles to Trooper
> Spring, a nice spot.
>
> Had one stretch today of six miles with no inter-
> mediate milestones—no trail junctions, views or lakes—
> and I found it very difficult to keep plodding along
> through forest.
>
> *Ann's journal:* The camp here is on the edge of quite
> a large meadow. Grass grows shoulder-high, and the
> spring is cold and deep.
>
> We'll do our twenty miles tomorrow instead of
> today.

We spent a few minutes talking with a couple who had
started on the Trail four days ago at Timberline and were
hiking south to Crater Lake. Their parents were meeting
them at each road crossing, and bringing along the couple's
ten-month-old baby to visit with them. The woman had both
knees wrapped. She said she was in discomfort and was hoping that she could buy more aspirin at Olallie Resort.

To cheer them up, we told them of my troubles with
my cramping leg, and of our problems with blisters. I don't
know if it helped *them*, but it sure raised *our* spirits to realize
that we actually were past those difficult days!

AUGUST 17

Log: 19.1 miles, from Trooper Spring to Clackamas Lake Campground.
Cold morning, hot afternoon, with wind from north. Mosquitoes
down; flies up.

Ann's journal: Today we hiked almost twenty miles
—our longest day since coming into Mazama Campground at Crater Lake, and also our first car campground since then, too. We came in the "back way,"
on the Trail, and we're not going to bother to walk
out to the front entrance to see how much this
place costs!

Boy, it was cold this morning at Trooper Spring.
Lee laughed at me, sitting huddled on a log, my nose
red, my hands around my cocoa cup, and I suppose
I must have looked a sight! Taking the tarp down
is always cold on the hands, and by the time we
were ready to leave we were both very cold. It
took us an hour to eat and break camp, and probably took an hour's worth of walking to warm up again.

Today's hiking was mostly through viewless but
pleasant forest, with about two major climbs and
corresponding long descents. Yesterday we discussed
the mail we'd each received, but today we walked
through many long silences.

Lee's journal: The trail was in good condition, but
lacked anything to hold our interest: no lakes and
few views. Made for a long day. Our pace has
picked up since the trail is in such good shape and
with a gentle grade.

We are both tired of hiking and need a break
from the routine. At least we are still nice to each

other. Ann takes good care of me, and I hope she feels the same about how I treat her.

This is our 12th straight day of hiking.

AUGUST 18

Log: 14.9 miles, from Clackamas Lake Campground to Lower Twin Lake. Hot, light wind, clear sky.

After leaving Clackamas Lake Campground early the next morning, we hiked around forested Timothy Lake, crossed its outlet stream on a boardwalk, and took a short side trip to "Little Crater Lake." This natural artesian spring was forty-five feet deep and crystal clear. We spent a long rest break here admiring its turquoise waters.

Ann's journal: For lunch we stopped at a seeping spring that was difficult to find. We had to hunt for it, and Lee finally located it in a jumble of moss and rhododendron. It looked like a big mud puddle, but with water clear and cold.

Lee's journal: We were able to see Mount Hood for part of the afternoon, so much closer than it was several days ago from the ridge north of Jefferson Park. We ended today at Lower Twin Lake, which is not much bigger than a pothole, and warm—unappealing to drink. The campsites here are messy from too much use by people who don't care.
Tomorrow we hope to reach Timberline Lodge. I'd like to get a room there for the night, and a *hot shower* and *food*.
Thirteen days.

Ann's journal: We haven't done a laundry since Summit Lake and our clothes are really suffering. It takes a long time to wash out two sets of hiking clothes and two sets of dirty socks in our little pot, and we just haven't scheduled a "wash day." My clothes are going to fall right off me in tatters!
This is a pretty lake, but the water is warm and slimy, probably the worst water we've had so far.

Ascending the slopes of Mount Hood.

AUGUST 19

Log: 8.8 miles, from Lower Twin Lake to Timberline Lodge. Temperature moderate. Clouds moving in from southwest.

Ann's journal: We did it! We're at Timberline Lodge on Mount Hood, which seemed so far away only a few days ago. It seemed far away even this morning as we walked through the forest way below. But by 11am we had covered the miles, and were standing at the lodge desk. Coming in on a Friday in mid-summer with no reservations, we happily took whatever was available and ended up with a cozy little room under the eaves, with a window looking south toward Mount Jefferson, which we could see until clouds covered it this afternoon.

Lee's journal: I left quite a ring in the tub just from taking a shower! After we got cleaned up, we went to the cafeteria for lunch. I had two half-pound hamburgers, Ann had a cheeseburger, and we had frozen yogurt for dessert. Then a swim in the pool, followed by a visit to the Blue Ox tavern for some wine (for me; 7-Up for Ann) and snacks, and after that we sat in the upstairs lounge to admire the mountain and enjoy some more wine (for me). It's been fun to play tourist.

We took advantage of having a telephone nearby. I called the company that made my boots to see if they would send me a new pair. They wouldn't, so I called home to ask that my extra boots be sent to Cascade Locks. Lee called his parents and sister, who said they would drive to Cascade Locks to meet us. He gave them a list of things to bring— including peanut butter for me, and food in general for Lee.

> *Ann's journal:* We splurged on an absolutely elegant dinner in the Lodge dining room this evening. I am now too sleepy to keep my eyes open. Lee is reading a Louis L'Amour western.

Although it was a luxury to spend a night in civilized surroundings once again, neither of us had a restful night.

> *Lee's journal:* I finished the western about 11:30pm, and had a rough night trying to sleep because of the clanking ice machine in the next room, singing in the lounge, barking of the lodge dog, and a noisy parking lot. Our list of Places Not To Camp now includes "rooms next to ice machines."

I fell sound asleep and was undisturbed by the ice machine and all the other distractions, but I was awakened about 4am by a peculiar dream that left me wide-eyed and strange-feeling. Not certain what to do with myself, I went for a walk through the sleeping hotel, startling the night manager when I padded sock-footed through the lobby. After the dream-feelings subsided, I was able to go back to sleep.

AUGUST 20

Log: 11.8 miles, from Timberline Lodge to Muddy Fork. Temperature cool, with clouds, occasional wind.

> *Ann's journal:* Before we left Timberline, I called the kids to make sure they were alright. Apparently the worst that's happened is that Marshall has fallen off his horse Smoky two times. Both he and Amber sounded happy and busy and it was nice to make contact with them.
>
> After reading the newspaper and having some more to eat, we finally convinced ourselves that it was Time To Go. We started hiking about noon, came into camp just after 6:30—but only did 11½ miles

by the book. Neither of us quite agrees with that, but we don't have any other figures to go by.

Lee's journal: This is Number Fifteen without a break.

By now Lee and I had tired of our daily routine of cold-water baths. Lee would sometimes bribe himself with promises of wine or other goodies at the next supply stop to make his bath easier to endure. I was not so good at silent suffering, however, and often complained loudly about the situation.

This evening as I was balking at having glacier water thrown on me for what passed as a "bath," Lee reminded me, "Peanutbutter at Cascade Locks!" which made me laugh and *did* make the icy shower easier to take.

After hiking the ups and downs of the Mount Hood Canyons, we were glad to stop at Muddy Fork to set up camp. By stepping out onto the rocks of the river bed, we could get a good view of the west side of Mount Hood above us. I built a fire after camp was set up, and we cooked our dinner by its light.

AUGUST 21

Log: 17.9 miles from Muddy Fork to Indian Spring. Moderate temperatures, some clouds.

Ann's journal: This morning we started right out with crossing three channels of the Muddy Fork, the first one on precarious logs that Lee *crawled* over on all fours. I would love to have had a photo of that, as to see that big, strong man crawl across these bridges looks so funny, but I never think of my camera until *I'm* safely across, too!

We had lovely views of Mount Hood as we walked around its west side, and at the junction of the PCT and the Round-the-Mountain Trail, we saw a note stuck on a signpost. It's always fun to read other people's "trail mail" and I had no compunctions about looking at it—imagine my surprise when I saw it was addressed "Ann and Lee." It was for us! Turns out that Mary Ann and Cliff were hiking around Mount Hood and had hoped to run into us, but missed us by two days. It sure made our morning to come across their note.

Lee's journal: When we set out today, we were aiming for Wahtum Lake, about 20 miles away, so we could get to Cascade Locks on Monday with no problem. But Ann ran out of steam in the late afternoon, and the trail got rough over rocks on Indian Mountain, so we called it a day at 18 miles. We'll still try for Cascade Locks tomorrow so we can take a *real* layover day on Tuesday. This is our sixteenth day of continuous hiking.

Ann's journal: Indian Springs is rather a miserable spot. Accessible by road, it has some dirty picnic tables and grubby fire pits, not much level space and no privacy.

Because we haven't been bothered by mosquitoes for the last several days, we decided to use just bivvy bags tonight to make the chores a little easier. So what do we have here? Mosquitoes! Also some little flies which are a nuisance.

The huckleberries around camp are ripe and delicious and we have eaten several of the choicest ones we could find. They are sweet and very juicy.

From a viewpoint this morning we could see Mount Adams and Mount Rainier in the distance! We're almost home! Later this afternoon, about a mile from camp, we could also see Saint Helens. What a delight to be able to see these familiar mountains.

AUGUST 22 and 23

Log: 16.1 miles from Indian Spring to Cascade Locks. Hot and clearing.

Lee's journal: We got an early start for Cascade Locks. At Wahtum Lake I noticed the focus ring for the 35-70mm zoom lens is not operating; don't know what happened to it. It will still focus, but not by turning the ring.

Ann's journal: We put in a 16-mile day from Indian Spring to Cascade Locks, first going up and down to Benson Plateau, and then dropping several thousand feet to the Columbia River. For a pack that wasn't supposed to have much in it, said Lee, his sure was heavy!

Lee's journal: We headed down on the Ruckel Creek Trail, shorter than other alternate routes described in the guidebook. We thought it would save us a couple of miles. It proved to be less than perfect: *too* steep, and very difficult with full packs. We slipped and fell in places.

Ann's journal: When we got to the bottom, we still had a couple of miles to walk into Cascade Locks. But there were ripe blackberries along the way and I was so hungry and thirsty I gobbled them by the handful.

Lee's journal: We walked right to the Visitor's Center at the Locks, thinking that we would camp at their campground. We read the PCT log book kept at the Visitor's Center, and made our own entry in it. The campground, unfortunately, is just an open field. Okay for tents, but not for us with a tarp.

I decided we should stay in a motel, and we hauled our packs back to the Scandian Motel, which is very comfortable and nice.

We really felt as though we were "on vacation" in Cascade Locks. We enjoyed every relaxing minute we spent there. Reaching this point in our hike was a real accomplishment—we had walked through the entire state of Oregon! We had been

Bridge of the Gods over the Columbia River.

hiking for about five weeks and had come about 450 miles from the Oregon/California border.

In the morning, we met Lee's parents and his sister, Sharon, who helped us repack from the supply boxes we picked up at the Post Office. We stuffed ourselves on the picnic lunch they had brought with them. Lee discovered there was no barber shop in the little town, so his folks drove us to Hood River so he could get a haircut. We looked through camera stores for another 35-70mm zoom lens, but came up zero. Lee would have to make do with a broken focus ring.

My replacement boots arrived at the Post Office, and I boxed up the other ones to send back to the manufacturer. I also received a box of chocolate chip cookies from friends in California!

AUGUST 24

Log: 15.2 miles from Cascade Locks to Panther Creek. Hot with no wind. No shade along highway.

Setting out from Cascade Locks, our first obstacle was the crossing of the Bridge of the Gods. Lee has no love for bridges of any sort, and this one was a particular bedevilment.

> *Ann's journal:* The bridge has no sidewalk; one must walk right in the roadway with the traffic, and its entire surface is that awful grating with the gaping holes in it. I looked down once and realized I would certainly get dizzy (although heights don't bother me). The only way across was to look straight ahead—then the surface *appeared* solid—and keep walking.

On the Washington side of Bridge of the Gods.

Lee tackled it head-on and strode across with giant steps, not stopping until he reached the other side where he waited for me.

A sign at the end said, "Welcome to Washington." Here the PCT was not yet complete. The new portion of trail had been roughed-in, but rather than hazard a guess as to where that roughed-in route might take us, we chose to walk the alternate route, along the highway through the towns of Carson and Stevenson. Although Lee's father had offered to drive us from Cascade Locks to our next camp at Panther Creek, we declined, even though we would be hiking on the shoulder of a busy highway.

> *Lee's journal:* In Stevenson I had maple bars for the first time this trip—three of them, very fresh and very good. In Carson we stopped at a little drugstore for *real* chocolate milkshakes. I think all the sweets didn't set well (including pancakes for breakfast), because my stomach felt upset for several miles. Finally we stopped and I had some plain bread and some water, which seemed to help.

> *Ann's journal:* We came into camp about 5:30 after seven hours of walking, and wondered why we went so slowly. Our planned distance had been only 12.5 miles. Although we had stopped for photographs and goodies, our pace hadn't been *that* slow.

> It wasn't until Lee figured up the day's mileage that he discovered we actually had gone *15.2*, not *12.5!* Mystery solved.

AUGUST 25

Log: 17.3 miles from Panther Creek to Sheep Lake. Hot with no wind. Saw "University of Washington Bat Study" and "Experimental Forest" signs. Ripe wild strawberries.

> *Lee's journal:* Although we got a good start in the morning, our pace was slow going uphill—we had to gain the 4000 feet of elevation that we had dropped to cross the Columbia. I had to get used to forest walking again after walking the highway with sights and sounds to distract.

> After lunch Ann picked up the pace and we made it to Sheep Lake in good time. Originally we had been scheduled to camp at Blue Lake—a distance of 22.9 miles from Panther Creek—but we really can't

handle that kind of distance.

It looks as though we'll arrive at White Pass on August 31. Our next week's camps will be uncertain, however, since our schedule through this stretch is now thrown off.

Sheep Lake itself is not much of a spot for camping due to poor water quality. Again, we are "desperate hikers," drinking whatever we come across. The lake is shallow and stagnant with a muddy, murky shoreline, although the water really isn't any worse than some spots in Oregon.

AUGUST 26

Log: 18.7 miles, from Sheep Lake to Mosquito Lake outlet stream. Moderate weather.

Ann's journal: We woke up this morning with the tarp dripping with dew. Sleeping bags, ground cloths, everything damp. I hate having to put on wet clothes day after day. Nothing ever dries. I hate wet socks. Wet socks into wet boots that never dry. Yuck. And it's not even raining! What will I do when it *rains?*

The fog lifted and the dew eventually dried under a blue-and-white sky, but haze from forest fires prevented us from enjoying any views as we climbed up and over Berry Mountain. In a few miles we passed Blue Lake, and were just as glad we had not spent the night there. Although it was a pretty scene, we saw that the lake was situated in a natural weather funnel and—just as at South Mathieu Lake in Oregon—camping there would be extremely windy.

One of the bright spots in this 19-mile day was that we were passing through acres and acres of ripe huckleberries. Some of these fields were the traditional berry-picking grounds of the Yakima Nation, and we saw many families collecting baskets of the fruit. I helped myself to any hapless berries within reach, and tossed them down like a bear.

Today's mileage came on the heels of 17 miles the day before, and 15 the day before that. We were really covering ground, but we were pooped!

Lee's journal: My feet hurt almost as much as when we first started out in Oregon! Maybe we're pushing too much. More 12 to 15 mile days would be

Melt-water streams tumbled from Mount Adams' glaciers.

easier. This is *hard work*. We saw a group of Scouts from the town of Washougal out for a 50-mile hike today. They were spending a week at it, and we've done 50 miles in three days!

When we arrived at the Mosquito Lake outlet stream, where we had planned to camp, we found the sole campspot already occupied. After hiking 19 miles already, we were not about to continue any farther that day. Clearing away some of the underbrush, we simply created ourselves a campsite off the trail a short way.

It was at this spot that Lee came up with the brilliant idea of fixing pancakes for dinner. Because of the colder weather and strenuous hiking, we both had become ravenous. Fixing pancakes for breakfast was just too bothersome, so we were carrying plenty of unused pancake mix. Using his coffee cup as a mixing bowl, Lee fixed us each a couple of pancakes to go with dinner that night. They were an instant hit.

In the days to come, Lee would fry the pancakes in about a quarter-inch of shortening, and then sop up all the grease in

the pan with his pancakes to try to satisfy his body's craving
for fat.

AUGUST 27

Log: 14.3 miles, from Mosquito Lake outlet stream to White Salmon
Springs. Temperature warm; no wind. Rain in morning.

> *Ann's journal:* Today is my son's twelfth birthday.
> I thought of Marshall throughout the day, hoping
> that Ed and Susie are doing something to make his
> day special. When I mentioned it this morning, Lee
> said, "Let's hope he's having more fun than *Mom* is!"

> *Lee's journal:* Rain began this morning about 6am.
> Luckily it stopped in a couple of hours, but it was
> not very pleasant to break camp in the downpour.

Although we sometimes hiked for days without seeing
another soul, and we liked to camp in privacy, we always enjoyed talking to other hikers on the trail. What a strange and
wonderful assortment of people we ran into!

> *Ann's journal:* Before we had been out even 5 miles
> this morning we met another PCT hiker who had set
> his pack down in mid-trail to make some adjustments.
> Sometimes other people we meet are so close-mouthed,
> but this fellow was open and inquisitive. We had to
> interupt him so that we could ask *our* questions!

Our standard questions were invariably about trail conditions ahead. After that, if we had the time and inclination,
we also asked where the other people had started hiking from,
and how far were they going. Comments about the vagaries of
the weather, the reliability of equipment, and the nearest
restaurant were all guaranteed conversation-starters with fellow
distance-hikers.

We knew that Mount Adams loomed ahead, but the weather
was not co-operating in providing us with views of this volcano.

> *Lee's journal:* We could only see the bottom half of
> Mount Adams today because of clouds. I'd hate to
> walk around it and not get to see it.
>
> It was nice to hike only 14 miles today and make
> camp early. Tonight the clouds look like more rain,
> with thunder off in the distance.

> *Ann's journal:* When we got to the springs, we found
> someone else camped here. Nice folks, but there's

only one campsite, so it meant we had to construct
our own for the second night in a row. Built a small
campfire tonight and now I've got *dry socks* to put
on tomorrow. Oh, the simple joys...

Have seen lots of deer tracks and a couple of deer
the last few days. Also a garter snake, grouse, and
lots of frogs. There are bear tracks occasionally on
the trail, but have not seen the animal yet. Have
seen two slugs total (one in Oregon).

AUGUST 28

Log: 16.5 miles, from White Salmon Springs to Muddy Fork. No bridge
over Middle Fork Adams River. Cool, windy; steady rain by afternoon.

Ann's journal: Didn't I write a couple of pages back,
"What will I do when it rains?" Well, it has rained
all afternoon and now I'm going to find out. It's a
little scary to think that we won't be heading home
to a wood stove and tea pot and dry clothes tonight.
Or tomorrow night. We must stay warm and we must
try to keep things dry. I have never had to stay out
in rain more than three days!

Where is the sun? Where are the blue skies? Where
is the heat I complained about?

Mount Adams.

We were lucky today to have good views of Mount Adams and its impressive glaciers before the summit was swallowed by a huge lenticular cloud. Flowers of every alpine variety were blooming their little hearts out and the hillsides were crammed with blue, orange, yellow, purple, white, and many shades of red. It gave me a lift to be in alpine country again. The PCT along the west side of Adams is easy trail and very enjoyable to walk.

Gusts of wind and spatters of rain made us stop once to get covers on our packs, and rain coats on us. Near Sheep Lake we met three older men. The first man was from Oklahoma and said he had come out every year for the last few years to hike a section of the PCT with his brother-in-law. He whipped out a little 110 camera and took our pictures!

The second man told us, with rain dripping off his coat, how the weather in Washington always held good until the autumnal equinox, so we'd better finish our trip by then.

The third man, whom we talked to while he was putting on his rain clothes, said, "Say, you're not the two hikers from Signpost, are you? We called up there for information, and they said we might run into you!" (Signpost, of course, is the magazine I work for; it is a well-known source of information for Northwest hikers.)

His recognition of us made us smile.

We walked 12 miles without a break, and then stopped to huddle in some trees for a quick bite of lunch. No boots-off, lie-against-a-log meal today.

Our camp is wet and sandy, but at least it's level.

Lee's journal: Last night's camp on sloping ground had me rolling into Ann every now and then. She would periodically push me back, and then I'd wake up. Had a difficult time sleeping.

Rain started again this afternoon and it has poured on us into the evening. No fire tonight; wet socks tomorrow. I don't know how Ann will be able to handle this wet travel; she doesn't seem to be doing too well now. Canada is a l-o-n-g way off if it rains on us the rest of the way, and it very well could.

The progress we are making on the map is very
satisfying. This trip is going to give me something
to look back on and feel good about.

AUGUST 29

Log: 15.6 miles, from Muddy Fork to Walupt Lake Trail junction. Rain
and cool with some wind.

Ann's journal: It rained all night. It rained all morning. The hiking was miserable. I sure wished there
had been a way to turn around and go home—but the
only way to get home is to keep going! Lee was
enormously helpful in keeping my confidence up,
saying, "We *can* make it; we *will* be all right."

Lee's journal: We found a small bag of Cheetos
alongside the trail by Midway, still intact and fresh.
We carried them along and shared them as a treat
for lunch. It made us wish we had a *big* bag!

Ann's journal: Just before lunch we saw another
human being out in this awful weather. He was
wearing denim jeans and a plastic raincoat, with no
pack cover, and his pack pockets unzipped and
collecting rain. We exchanged greetings with him,

It rained all night; it rained all morning.

Wringing out our socks became part of our regular routine.

and as soon as we were a few trees past him, we
grinned at each other and Lee got out the words
just as I was about to say them—"If *he* can make
it through the Goat Rocks, *we* can!"

We faced another psychological bugaboo that next day—
crossing the Goat Rocks Wilderness and the Packwood Glacier
at 7000 feet. The Goat Rocks has a reputation for fierce and
sudden storms at any time of the year. The PCT climbs up
and over its highest ridge well above timberline, with no trees
or even shrubs for protection from the elements.

I was nervous about the prospect of getting ourselves up
into that high country in this marginal weather and then getting
stuck: a white-out or snow storm or gale-force winds could
halt our progress. I knew that a young woman had lost her
life in this rugged country because of being caught in just such
a storm as I was afraid of. As we climbed tomorrow, we would
pass the memorial Dana Yelverton Shelter, erected in her name
by her family and church.

Lee's journal: This rain will get both of us down.
It doesn't take much to remind me of the misery
of the '78 trip with Dennis. Both Ann and I had
morale problems today. It would be a shame to

quit now—we really don't have that far to go, considering where we started.

I spent part of the day thinking over our supply
situation in case we must turn back or make an
emergency camp. We don't have much extra, but
we could survive an additional day if we had to.
We made an early camp (2:30pm) after covering
16 miles, since the next campsites were another 4
miles away. This spot is not very protected, and
we're getting wind blowing right through the tarp at
times. While gathering wood after setting up camp,
I found a better spot only a couple of minutes
farther down the trail. We should have spent more
time looking around. It doesn't help matters any
to have a poor camp.

Ann's journal: We tried drying our socks over the
MSR (our little backpacking stove) which sorta worked
after Lee wrung quarts of water out of them.

After dinner, the rain let up, so I decided to start
a small drying fire with some wood Lee had found
earlier. Our outer socks were still quite wet, and my
hiking shirt was so wet that I was dreading having to
force myself to wear it tomorrow. That shirt was
my first priority at the fire. Then Lee came to sit
by the fire to dry his socks a little more. It wasn't
long, though, before he left to climb into his sleeping bag to try to warm up. His feet were very cold
from putting the wet socks back on. I finally convinced him to put on a pair of dry socks (he's always
saving them for an "emergency") and after an hour
he said his feet felt "civilized" again.

Our campsite is windy and rain is being blown
around the corners of the tarp.

During the night we experienced a terrible rain storm. The
water came down in sheets; the wind blew it right in on us.
Luckily, our down sleeping bags were protected inside our bivvy
bags. We tossed and turned. Lee reported that he was awake
for two hours during the hardest of the rain.

Sometime in the middle of the night, I awoke feeling
"closed in." It took me a minute of struggling to realize that
I really *was* trapped—by the tarp! A huge bathtub of water
had collected right above me. As I shined my flashlight around,

I could see that the collapse of the bulge was iminent. When
it gave way, we would be flooded.

I scrambled out from beneath it and, while Lee supported
the bathtub from inside, I threw my rain clothes over my
pajamas, grabbed a cup, and dashed outside into the storm to
bail us out. Scoop after scoop, I gradually emptied the tarp of
its load.

We woke up several times that night to check for bulges,
but it didn't happen again.

AUGUST 30

**Log: 16.1 miles, from Walupt Trail junction to Mc Call Basin. Cool and
cloudy, sprinkles of rain.**

Lee's journal: We woke to grey and wet skies. Although
the wind and rain had stopped, the weather still looked
very threatening. We set out to cross the Goat Rocks
after breakfast, not expecting to see anyone else. Just
below Cispus Pass, we picked out a figure coming
toward us through the fog: a PCT hiker who had
started from Snoqualmie Pass and who had spent the
night at the Yelverton Shelter. He hadn't seen anyone else on the trail today.

After we crossed Cispus Pass, we began to see fresh
tracks on the trail—going our way! We couldn't
figure out who it might be.

As we were eating lunch out of the wind at the
Shelter, a group of five or six came in. They were
spending a week hiking from White Pass to Walupt
Lake, and told us that the footprints belonged to a
a PCT hiker headed for Canada. From their description, he must be the same fellow we talked to at
Cascade Locks, now only a few miles ahead of us.

Although it was cool, and rain sprinkled on us, the
weather wasn't too bad. Climbing up above timberline, we
walked through fields of flowers, still brilliant under the grey
skies, and every now and then we caught a glimpse of the rows
of jagged peaks above us in the clouds. In spite of the not-
perfect weather, we thought the Goat Rocks Wilderness was
beautiful—another place we wanted to come back to.

After passing the Yelverton Shelter, we climbed to the
ridge, somewhat dreading the crossing of the Packwood Glacier.
We had heard stories of how hikers and horses lost their
footing on the steep ice, to fall to death or injury far below.

Our fears were unfounded. Although quite steep, the "glacier"
at this time of year was nothing more than four small remnant
snowfields with a well-used track booted across them. We
could understand that this would be a dangerous spot, particu-
larly early in the summer when the snow fields would be large,
and when the snow would be ice-hard and difficult to walk on;
however, we crossed it easily.

Descending the north side of the Goat Rocks, we found
the trail not very well marked, and several times we consulted
our maps at intersections. Many trees were down across the
trail, making side trails into the woods necessary to get around
them. Here also, the PCT had been re-routed. Although we
had intended to stay on the new trail, somehow we got off
on the old one and ended up in Mc Call Basin. It seemed
like a lovely place to camp, so we stayed for the night.

> *Ann's journal:* We both had problems today with
> volcanic ash working into our socks; we both have
> sore places where it has rubbed on our skin. (For
> several days we had been hiking and camping on
> several inches of ash from the 1980 eruption of
> Mount Saint Helens.)
>
> The skies have cleared tonight, stars are out and
> the temperature has dropped. We won't have another

Crossing the Goat Rocks—above timberline and under grey skies.

rain storm. But we *do* have mice here. I surprised one right in my pack after dinner.

Lee's journal: Rain four out of seven days! But as we were heading up the trail this morning we saw a rainbow. Perhaps our luck with weather will change. It is so nice to have no wind, no rain, and a pleasant campsite again. Even Ann's morale is improving.

AUGUST 31

Log: 9.5 miles from Mc Call Basin to White Pass. No rain! Overcast and cool.

In the morning we discussed how to get back on the main trail from Mc Call Basin. Since we weren't sure how we got to Mc Call Basin in the first place, the route back out seemed elusive. Each of us wanted to go a different way. Finally, after bringing out the map and compass, Lee convinced me that his way would be successful. Dubiously, I followed him, and sure enough, in a mile or so we came upon a junction with the Pacific Crest Trail.

> *Lee's journal:* Due to having to gain a thousand feet and stopping for pictures, along with an early lunch at the ridge top above Shoe Lake, we really didn't go as fast as we normally would. Ann slows way down on steeper uphill stretches; it costs us in time, but she makes up for it in a fast downhill and level pace. Sometimes it gets difficult to plod behind her on steep uphills, since it is more comfortable for me to go faster and get it over with.
>
> On our way down Hogback Ridge, we met a couple from Oregon who were going into the Goat Rocks. During our exchange of information, they told us how to ride the chairlift down to White Pass. The man had never been on a chairlift before, and didn't like heights either, but he had managed to conquer the challenge, and he helped to bolster my confidence. Although I didn't like the idea of riding in a chairlift, it would save us about three miles of walking and would give us something different to do.

Reaching the top of the ski lift, we used the buzzer at the control building to contact the chairlift operator at the bottom of the hill. Making sure he knew that Lee was a "first-timer," we carefully loaded ourselves and our packs onto the chairlift.

I thought it was a marvelous ride: we could see the top of
Mount Rainier to the west, and what a luxury it was to just
sit and be transported!

> *Lee's journal:* I clung to the iron bar in the middle
> and to my pack and had my eyes shut most of the
> time. It seemed to take forever. I felt scared and
> uncomfortable, but I kept telling myself how good
> it was not to be hiking.
>
> When we got to the bottom, we walked over to
> the lodge, had some hamburgers, and then got a
> room for the night at the White Pass Inn.

We walked over to the Crackerbarrel General Store to
pick up our next supply box. As we walked in, the man
behind the counter said, "You must be Ann and Lee!" It was
nice to feel that we were expected. He offered us the space
in the foyer of the building to do our repacking, and we used
the coin-operated washing facilities there to do laundry.

> *Lee's journal:* We picked up groceries at the store—
> eggs, cheese, beer for me and root beer for Ann, a
> big bag of Cheetos, frozen pizza, orange juice, milk,
> bread, shortbread cookies, and ice cream bars—and
> went back to our room at the Inn. Ann used up
> all the hot water taking a shower, so I had to wait
> for mine. It began to rain again, but we were able
> to air some of our things before it started. Forest
> Service Ranger Mike Hiler from the Naches District
> came to visit and brought some fruit, and the fellow
> from the store came by to bring a package that had
> arrived after we had left.
>
> We didn't eat dinner until after 9pm, and stayed
> up very late. It was difficult to sleep in the stuffy
> motel room with the rain pounding down outside.
> And the alarm went off at 5:30am—I thought I had
> turned it *off!*

The Yelverton Shelter, above, and its inscription.

WHITE PASS TO STEVENS PASS

SEPTEMBER 1

Log: 13.3 miles, from White Pass, to a creek south of Fish Lake. Rain and wind. Trail a mud hole.

> *Ann's journal:* Being inside a building and warm and dry last night was great. Once we both got up and stood at the door to watch the sheets of rain pour

Although these downed trees have been cut into sections, they still block the trail, and we must bushwack around them.

down. It may very well do the same thing on us
tonight.

The trouble with motel rooms is you can never
get the temperature just right. Last night was hot
and stuffy as Lee had determined there was no way
to open the window. He discovered the secret about
4 in the morning: brute force.

After a large breakfast, we walked over to the
lodge. While Lee had dessert, I called Snoqualmie
Pass to see if I could scrounge up a room somewhere.
I talked to the manager of the Alpenrose Condo, who
said she had a vacant unit we can stay in. So we
can look forward to a roof over our heads and hot
water in just a week.

Today on the trail we met a family of five hiking
from Chinook to White Pass. The man was very
cheerful and talkative, and the two-burner Coleman
stove he was carrying like a suitcase certainly was a
conversation-starter. Behind him came two little
boys, then in a minute the wife and daughter showed
up—the woman was carrying a gallon can of fuel for
the stove! Except for the man, all were in jeans and
sneakers.

The young woman on horseback

Lee's journal: He also had a
camera around his neck with
no case and no lens cover (in
the rain!) and the woman was
carrying around her neck a
pair of binoculars. He
appeared quite strong, so had
no problem carrying the
stove. They wanted a two-
burner, he said, so they could
easily cook food for the five
of them. He also said they
were new to backpacking.

Ann's journal: A short time
later we were overtaken by
a young woman on horseback
going solo to Chinook Pass
and back. She was very
friendly. We had seen her

earlier as we were walking down the road to the trailhead at White Pass—she drove by and offered us a ride. We saw her a couple of more times on the trail today as we leap-frogged along. She is camped somewhere ahead of us, and we will probably see her again as she heads back in a day or two.

We were going to try to make up one of our late-days on this section, but we didn't leave White Pass until after 11am this morning, and we stopped about 2 miles short of our intended camp this afternoon. We're at a very comfortable creekside camp, much used. I got chilled as soon as we stopped hiking, and even though I put on my jacket and hat right away, I was cold and lethargic for some time, enough for Lee to ask if I were all right and to keep an eye on me.

We noted the other day that although Lee has more tolerance for things like cold baths, he suffers from the cold longer, and while I complain loudly about having glacier water poured over me, I recover much faster.

It is dismal and depressing to set up camp in the rain, but comforting when it is done. We are getting pretty good at putting our "house" together.

It rained off and on the entire day. Our logbook noted that the trail was "a mudhole." Although the path rambled through pretty country, we would have to come back to appreciate it sometime when it was not raining.

SEPTEMBER 2

Log: 19.5 miles, from south of Fish Lake to Sheep Lake. Cold. Fog. Rain. Wind.

Ann's journal: In the morning we packed up a wet tarp and started off in rain clothes—our "dress-du-jour" since we have been in Washington. Just a few minutes down the trail we ran into our gal on the horse. She was headed out! She told us she didn't know what she had done wrong, but she sure got wet last night, and wet toilet paper this morning was the last straw; she was going home! She wished us luck and rode off into the mist. Since we had started on the trail at 7:30am, and she had camped well ahead of us, she must have been up at first light to load up and be off.

The clouds were thick and low and mostly rained on us all morning. I hike in my rain coat with a flannel shirt underneath, and I am usually soaked from condensation and sweat not long after I warm up. The rain coat acts as a "wet suit" and at least keeps me warm as long as I am moving. A wool hat helps on the downhill sections where I am not burning so many calories. I can't stand the feel of clammy rain pants on my legs, so I just wear gaiters. Lee strolls along behind in full rain gear: he needs both the rain pants and jacket to stay warm.

The weather today was just miserable. No glorious views of Mount Rainier. No expansive meadows of flowers: they were all dripping wet and unattractive.

By the time we got to Dewey Lakes the rain had stopped. We took off our packs in a little mosquito-infested boggy meadow just before the lakes for a break—only our second one of the day. I finally got out my camera, which Lee had been urging me to do all day. He'd been taking pictures right along, just as though the sun were out.

On the climb out of Dewey Lakes we both got roaring hot and the rain jackets finally came off. We crossed right over Chinook Pass without stopping and kept going right to Sheep Lake. A whopping 19½ miles by 4 in the afternoon.

Lee's journal: We are both getting fed up with the weather. We can't dry our towels or clothes on the backs of our packs as we used to. We are starting to struggle with wet and cold camps. Part of the problem is wind coming around the edge of the tarp.

We saw several deer and an elk today—some consolation for not seeing Rainier.

Ann's journal: Only one other fellow is camped here, across the lake. We have a reasonable campsite, a little slanty, but not bad. We heated water to wash in tonight because we were so cold we couldn't bear the thought of another cold bath.

We discussed what we might do differently to stay warmer, but didn't come up with too many ideas

except to stay out of the wind. Tonight is bitter
cold; we can see our breath in steam clouds.

SEPTEMBER 3

Log: 16 miles, from Sheep Lake to Arch Rock Shelter. Cool, fog, and
     rain.

Lee's journal: We had blue skies this morning in spite
of the wind. We even got a tiny glimpse of Mount
Rainier, although it didn't last long; fog and clouds
moved in.

Ann's journal: It is getting *tiresome* to have no views
in an area where views are spectacular. Not only
that, it is *tiresome* to have wet socks and wet boots
and wet hiking clothes. And also to have no dry
place to *sit*, and mist blowing into everything.

Lee's journal: In Little Crow Basin we stopped to
talk with two PCTers hiking to Seiad Valley in
California. They had spent the previous night at
Arch Rock Shelter with two north-bound PCTers—
one of them was the guy we met at Cascade Locks,
and the other must be the fellow he had hoped to
catch up with. They told us the shelter was nice,
and Ann was looking forward to staying there. But
when we arrived it was already occupied by a young
couple. Although they offered to share the little
cabin with us, we decided to set up the tarp in the
adjacent woods.

They told us that on Thursday a plane had been
shot down by Russia and that Senator Jackson had
died. The story sounds far-fetched and we're not
sure what to make of it.

Ann's journal: This couple told us that they come to
the Arch Rock Shelter every year for Labor Day.
I practically drooled as I watched her make thick
cheese sandwiches for her and her husband as their
dinner of stew bubbled on the fire. And they had
root beer, too—I am envious.

We have a nice spot for the tarp, and a crackling
little fire. But everything is dark and damp and hung
with great ropes of moss. We agreed that it must
never be summer here.

It seems just a few minutes ago Lee was saying,

"Gee, it's only 6:40," and I replied, "We could be in bed in half an hour if we get these dishes washed." So we *did* get the dishes washed, and things picked up, and the tarp organized, and the maps looked at, and a few minutes of conversation, and watching some deer play in the woods—how did it get to be 8 o'clock and dark out?

Lee has just lost his toothbrush! It's not anywhere around. The tarp is strung low because of the rain, so things are cramped in here. Searching for anything is difficult. Disaster was averted; he borrowed my toothbrush. We'll look for his in the morning when it's light.

SEPTEMBER 4

Log: 14.3 miles, from Arch Rock Shelter to Green Pass. Cool, misty, windy.

Ann's journal: Found Lee's toothbrush. This morning everything was damp and misty, same as last night. With the tarp so low, I feel I am crammed into the attic! I much prefer nice weather. We left Arch Rock about 8am, while the couple in the shelter was still asleep with their bread and their cheese and their radio.

Several large blowdowns covered sections of the PCT through here; some of them were so extensive that they re-

Starting a fire at Green Pass.

quired long side trails to circumvent. Some had to be climbed over; a real nuisance, we agreed, especially in the damp, misty weather and with a very muddy trail.

Ann's journal: We met a couple of men toting muzzleloaders, carrying leather packs, and looking generally backwoodsy. They let us heft their rifles to see how heavy they were.

Lee's journal: Later in the day we met a couple hiking from Stampede Pass to Chinook Pass who had stayed the night at Green Pass. The information they gave us convinced us that we should plan to stay there, too, even though it would make only a 14-mile day. From what they told us, the camps after Green Pass lacked trees—something that we need to set up the tarp!

Ann's journal: We had a fire this evening and I dried my socks.

Water here is from a spring about a quarter-mile away (it seems longer) on elk trails that take off straight down the west side of the pass. I made two trips down for water—the first time not really knowing where I was going, the second time feeling more confident.

When I came up from the second trip, Lee was talking with a hiker! Darned if people don't pop up in the strangest places. His name is Jerome, from Chicago. He has been picking out my boot pattern in the mud since before White Pass—he and I are both wearing Galibiers.

Lee's journal: Ann seems a little grumpy. This section has been tough because of weather. We're just going one day at a time.

Ann's journal: I always forget all the things I think of during the day that I want to put down here. Too cold and sleepy. I think we're under a flight path. Last night it was owls keeping me awake—tonight it's jets!

SEPTEMBER 5

Log: **19.2 miles from Green Pass to Lizard Lake. Mist and rain clearing to sun and blue sky. Windy and cool.**

The sun came out and we could see Mount Rainier!

Ann's journal: This morning we woke in a cold, blowing mist that dripped from the trees and condensed onto everything. All of our gear feels damp. I was able to warm up after we'd been hiking for a while, but Lee stayed cold for a long time and I was watching him for hypothermia symptoms. It could easily have happened in weather like today. We've been lucky so far not to have had any problems.

About mid-morning, after we were thoroughly miserable and wet, and I had slipped in the mud, the mists lifted and the *sun* came out for the rest of the day! Amazing what a change it makes—we could see! Mount Rainier came out and all the Alpine Lakes peaks and the entire Stuart Range. The sun helped warm up Lee and made me drip with sweat. So we survived the day.

Lee's journal: The blue sky had a definite effect on our attitudes, and we made good time through the clear-cuts. We passed, and were passed by, Jerome at times today.

Ann's journal: When we stopped for lunch I spread out some things to dry. How we will make it to

Canada if it turns wet and cold again is beyond me.

We anticipated coming into a little forest lake with a few woodsy campsites, but what we ended up with is a little reed-filled pond with no campsites. And this at the end of a 19-mile day! We walked another quarter-mile past the lake to an old road bed up on a bank, which we declared "home."

"A real psychological let-down," said Lee.

We got our water from the lake's outlet stream, and are treating it with a double-dose of iodine.

Lee's journal: We're going to try to make it to Snoqualmie Pass tomorrow. It means another 19-mile day, but I want to get some food and dry out.

Despite our camp being on a "road bank and rocky and slope-y," as Lee wrote, we made it fairly comfortable. The skies were clear during the night and we woke up in the early morning to see the constellation Orion glowing above—a sure sign of approaching winter.

SEPTEMBER 6 and 7

Log: 20.5 miles from Lizard Lake to Alpenrose Condominiums at Snoqualmie Pass. Cool with light wind; rain in afternoon.

Although we left Lizard Lake in sunshine and had a pleasant morning with views of Rainier, ripe huckleberries, and blue skies, by mid-day the clouds moved in and began to rain.

Lee's journal: Our spirits had been high as we left camp, but sank with the weather as we neared the pass. The last seven miles we hiked in rain, mist and fog.

Ann's journal: After lunch I tried to pick up my pace a bit; I am concerned that Lee is cold even while hiking. He hasn't an ounce of fat left; all the calories he consumes go toward immediate fueling.

Past Olallie Meadows we left the clearcuts and were in forest again. Lots of mud, rocks and roots in the trail. I was getting tired and frustrated trying to negotiate the obstacles. And something was wrong with my shoelaces—they were trying to do me in. Twice I tripped when the loop of one lace caught the hook of the opposite boot. Then the loop snagged on the rough edge of a log, and I was nearly on my face in a mudhole! My mood was so black by this time that I don't think I even thanked Lee when he came to my rescue and unsnagged me. I just got up with mud all over my hands where I'd caught myself, and stomped on through the goop.

Lee's journal: From Beaver Lake at the top of the ski hill, the PCT seemed to meander and take us away from the pass. Being in no mood for more wet trail than necessary, we cut straight down the ski slope.

Arriving at the highway by the Continental Restaurant, we had to walk a quarter-mile east to the Rock Chalet to pick up our supply box at the general store and post office. Expecting to be able to re-pack right in the store as we had done at White Pass, we were surprised when we were told we could not—we would have to cross the highway and repack in the public restroom building. So in the rain we had to lug not only our packs but also three boxes across a busy highway.

The box from my sister contained chocolate chip cookies, homemade bread, lollipops, peanut butter, jam, raisins, and garlic powder. We ate the bread and cookies as we repacked.

Ann's journal: Actually, the public restroom building wasn't all that bad—a big, well-lit lobby, warm and dry with plenty of space to spread out all our things. To get our return box of film, maps, and guidebook pages back to the post office before it closed, we hurried through our packing. Lee was getting anxious about the time; we were both tired and grouchy. With full and heavy packs, we hurried back to the post office to mail the box.

Lee's journal: Then we bought a few things for dinner: tortillas, margarine, soda, wine, cookies, Cheetos, ice cream, beer, bread, eggs, cheese, bacon, and orange juice.

The next chore was getting to the condominium, a walk of about 1½ miles. We were not certain where it was, and walking in the rain along the highway with a sack of groceries at the end of a long day with short tempers didn't help any.

We cut right down the Snoqualmie Summit ski slope.

I walked fast and Ann tried her best to keep up. Part way the bag began to fall apart.

Ann's journal: Out rolled the orange juice. When I reached it I called to Lee to stop, but he didn't hear me. Called and called, but he was striding along as fast as he could. Then out came another can. And another. When I reached them, I stuck them in my coat pocket. Finally he heard me shouting, and adjusted the bag.

Lee's journal: I had not realized what was happening. I can imagine the sight from someone's house as they watched two figures in the rain, one striding ahead, the other falling behind, as cans dropped one by one! Arriving finally at the condominium, we couldn't find the way in—all the doors were locked. I sat in the covered garage while Ann went searching. It was nice to be out of the rain even though I was in a garage, and I started thinking how we would spend the night there if we couldn't find the manager.

In a while, Ann came back with the manager, who took us to our room.

The next day we walked—leisurely, this time—back to the store for postcards, more groceries, and stove fuel. On the way there we stopped at the Continental Restaurant for cinnamon rolls. On the way back we stopped at the restaurant again for lunch.

In between drying our gear and washing our clothes, we sat around with our feet up, drank our beer and root beer, and read newspapers. We enjoyed a visit from three of my co-workers, Charlie, Eileen, and Plum, who brought us pizzas, more wine, and some wonderful brownies that my father had made and sent along with them. They also brought an extra wool shirt for Lee which he hoped would keep him warmer while hiking.

The condo manager brought us a huge section of her European fruit pie, with a delicious sauce to go with it. She even gave us laundry soap to do our laundry in the condo's washing facilities. She also told us that the weather forecast was for rain to continue through the week.

SEPTEMBER 8

Log: 14.8 miles from Snoqualmie Pass to Park Lake Basin. Rain, fog, snow, and cold.

Lee's journal: It seems we spent the whole day doing nothing but climbing out of Snoqualmie Pass. It rained occasionally, and other times we had fog and drizzle, with a few patches of sun. At higher elevations it even snowed on us; it is *very* cold.

Ann's journal: I almost fell asleep just now, snuggled down in my bag to get warm. Lee has been writing away industriously for some time. I am curious what our different journals will say when this trip is done.

"Camp" tonight is just a level spot on top of some blueberries, reasonably protected from wind but very wet. No fire tonight. Wet socks, wet boots, and wet clothes tomorrow. And probably a damp sleeping bag.

SEPTEMBER 9

Log: 14.7 miles from Park Lake Basin to Waptus Lake. Snow, rain and gloom in morning; sun in afternoon. Cool with light wind.

Ann's journal: I was toasty warm and dry through all the storm last night, waking only occasionally when a rain squall came through. Early this morning I woke and looked out onto the meadow. It was so bright I thought a full moon was shining. But no—about an inch of snow had fallen! We just snuggled a little deeper in our bags and waited for daylight.

When Charlie was visiting us at Snoqualmie Pass, he casually mentioned that we should consider the Waptus Pass Trail as an alternate to climbing over Escondido Ridge.

Lee's journal: We were concerned about the Ridge since camp spots on it are not well-protected, and we were scheduled to be camped on it at the same elevation as Park Lake Basin. Considering the snow we were in, we decided to take Charlie's alternate.

Ann's journal: And I'm glad we did. The mileage was about the same, but we're farther along by avoiding the long climb up to 5500 feet. The Waptus Pass Trail took us by Pete Lake, where we had lunch and the sun came out, and through a ford of Lemah

Climbing up from Snoqualmie Pass in the fog.

Waptus Lake from Waptus Pass.

Creek, and up one side of Waptus Pass and down the other to Waptus Lake, which is huge and has many campsites.

How nice to have a ready-made camp, with a level spot for the tarp, and a fire ring with a bench to sit on! We have a huge, spacious camp right by the lake. No wind, the sky is clear (well, mostly) and the bed is comfortable.

Lee's journal: I tried fishing and had one on with the first cast of a Super-duper, but the fish got away. On the third cast the lure hooked on a deep submerged log and I had to break the line. Damn! I had wanted to do a lot more fishing with it. Tried other lures and flies with no success. I'd like to come back and spend some time seriously fishing.

The next section contains a glacier stream Ann has heard stories about. Unfortunately, she told me too—now we're both concerned. If it isn't one thing, it's another.

At least for tonight we have one of the nicest campsites we've had the whole trip. Since we don't have far to go tomorrow, we probably will even sleep in a little. Having a fire tonight reminded me of beach hikes when we would spend hours by the fire talking.

Ann's journal: Tried to dry my socks very gently but absolutely scorched them. Now I'm down to two pairs of socks.

We spent a very relaxing evening by the fire. What a contrast to the stark, edge-of-hypothermia situation we were in last night!

Little did we realize that the next day we would *really* learn what "survival situation" meant.

SEPTEMBER 10

Log: 12.1 miles from Waptus Lake to Cathedral Rock. Flood.

Ann's journal: This has been the most *miserable* day I have *ever* spent hiking, except for tomorrow, which probably will be worse. If we survive to reach Stevens Pass we shall be fortunate.

Lee's journal: Rain began in the wee hours of the morning and has continued ever since. What a disappointment to awake to rain and foul weather after such a nice afternoon and evening.

All the while hoping the rain would quit, we didn't get started until 9am. We set out with poor attitudes. Ann especially was unhappy.

Ann's journal: This was not the kind of rain that comes in showers; no—it has been a steady, hard rain, occasionally increasing to a downpour. All day. The trails were absolutely running with water, the brush was sopping, and mud holes were frequent. Miles and miles of this we did, climbing to Deep Lake.

After only a few hours, the creeks had swollen to rushing torrents. Footlogs and stepping stones had disappeared. Below Deep Lake, I tried inching across a branch of Spinola Creek on a spindly, swaying pole. I slipped and fell in. Sat right down in the creek, pack and all.

Lee came to my rescue, although he was *not* happy about coming halfway back across the creek to reach me as he had already crossed safely by a different route. That I was doused with creek water didn't matter by now, since my coated nylon rain gear was completely inadequate for these conditions; it had "failed" and I was soaked to the skin anyway. Lee's Gore-tex coat had also "failed" and he was as wet as I.

Lee's journal: When we reached Deep Lake I was in

the lead and followed what I thought was the trail.
It went along the wrong side of the lake through
swamp and marsh and I didn't realize the mistake
until we were halfway around the lake. Hauling
out the map, we discovered we had gone wrong;
then we had to go back over that miserable trail.

> *Ann's journal:* We had to figure out how to cross
> the Deep Lake outlet, normally an easy rock-hop.
> But with the flood waters rising, we crossed with
> difficulty on the few rocks that were left.
>
> We met six people on the trail—two horsemen
> heading out; a man and a woman ready to cut
> their trip short and head out; and two gals at Deep
> Lake, heading out. We can't "head out;" we just
> keep "heading north!"

We climbed to Cathedral Pass in the downpour, hiking
along a trail which itself had turned to a streambed. Water
sloshed in my boots and ran down my neck. We were warm
only as long as we kept moving. For "lunch" we gobbled one
of Lee's energy bars, washing it down with a swallow of water
as we stood in the trail.

We called it a day after twelve miles in the storm, and
set up camp at 2:30pm by a stream on the north side of
Cathedral Rock. As soon as we stopped hiking we both were
cold and shivering. We were aware that this was a dangerous
time—both of us wet, both cold, and perfect hypothermia
weather. In our urgency to set up a protective camp, we had
little patience with each other.

> *Lee's journal:* I tried to set up Ann's extra poncho
> to protect our packs while we unloaded them, but
> I got upset by the weird size of it—too narrow to
> do much good.
>
> *Ann's journal:* Stringing up the poncho started out
> as a good idea, but Lee ended up shouting at me,
> which I didn't appreciate.

Shelter was a priority, and we set up the main tarp as
quickly as possible. Next was getting out of wet clothes and
into "less-wet" garments. We had to start from the skin out,
as even our underwear was drenched. We then pulled on a
warming, if not-quite dry, layer of wool.

The little stream by our camp was now a nearly uncross-
able torrent. Its one footlog was awash and looked as though

it would be swept away any minute. A little gully near our camp that had been dry when we arrived suddenly became a raging watercourse. As the afternoon passed and the rainstorm continued, we watched in amazement as every little ditch and hollow became a running creek. Waterfalls appeared from the cliffs on Cathedral Rock above us, and thundered down into the basin. We hoped we were on high enough ground to escape the flood.

With camp finally set up, warm clothes on, and ruffled feathers smoothed, we took shelter in our tarp and had an official lunch with hot drinks. The next day we had planned to face the crossing of the infamous Mount Daniel glacier stream. Fed by ice fields high on Mount Daniel, the stream was said to be dangerous to cross. In such a storm, we discussed the possibility that we would not be able to ford it.

> *Lee's journal:* It looks like tomorrow we will back-track and take the alternate route to avoid the glacier stream. It will be longer and will cost us time, but it's too unsafe to try to ford an already questionable stream.
>
> My rain jacket and pants are wet inside and out. My wool shirt and pants are damp and my pack is sopping! We've been very careful, but it has rained so much—more than I have ever experienced out hiking. The rain is coming down even harder now! This is unbelievable. We can't continue in this weather. Either the sun has to come out, or we have to head out by the shortest route to seek shelter.

Not long after we finished lunch, we decided it was time for dinner. Spaghetti was on the menu. We boiled the noodles, washed the dishes, and cooked our tea by collecting rain water from the edge of the tarp. The run-off was so heavy that our pot filled in a matter of seconds. After dinner we spread out our bed things.

> *Ann's journal:* Our ground cloths are still wet from last night, but my sleeping bag has only one small wet spot from its dunking in Spinola Creek. Three cheers for plastic bags.
>
> How I wish I were home and warm and dry and safe, but wishing does no good now. It is important to be careful and stay calm.

That evening over tea we looked at the maps, deciding

which way the closest road was, which direction we should go
the next day to end the hike, to seek civilization and safety.

As dusk fell, a tremendous thunderclap resounded through
the little basin, as a giant flash of lightning lit the sky. We
looked at each other with wide-eyed concern.

Lee's journal: Might be a long night.

SEPTEMBER 11

Log: 13.5 miles from "Rainstorm Camp" to Trap Lake. Cold with a
light wind—but no rain!

In the morning we poked our heads out of our cocoons
to discover the rain had stopped; we had survived the night!

> *Ann's journal:* Our hiking clothes were sopping, right
> down to the underwear. Putting on wet clothes would
> be no way to start the day, so I suggested we get a
> fire going and dry some of our gear. Using one of
> Lee's paraffin fire starters and a lot of very wet
> wood, we got a nice little blaze going after a while.

Lee tied a piece of tarp cord from tree to tree so it
would go right over the fire and we could hang wet clothes
on it to increase our drying efficiency. A lick of flame leaped
up and burned the cord right in two, dumping a load of clothes
into the fire. But it was all so wet that nothing burned!

> *Ann's journal:* We steamed our hiking clothes until
> they could be worn, and got most other things so
> they were only damp. Still, much in the packs re-
> mains wet.
>
> We finally left camp about 9:30. The little rush-
> ing stream in the gully had stopped running completely.
> The uncrossable torrent had its footlog askew, but
> was much reduced in volume. Seeing this change for
> the better, we took heart and decided to go for the
> Mount Daniel stream rather than turn around. Lee
> was anxious to face the monster, so he went ahead
> with his long stride. Soon he was out of sight and
> I was left with my own imagination about what we
> would face.
>
> I found Lee waiting at the stream, which was
> tumbling and crashing with a fearsome noise from
> way high above us. It looked deep and fast. Lee
> tested the depth with a stick and discovered it was

Looking down on Trap Lake.

less than a foot deep. It really wasn't very wide. Maybe this wouldn't be so bad after all!

Lee's journal: It *looked* impressive, but I was surprised how easy it was. We waded over in our boots; they were wet already. The stream was running very fast, but since it was shallow, the swiftness wasn't a problem.

Once across, we were much happier. We checked maps to make sure this was the "hard" one, then set off. The whole thing was similar to Russell Creek in Oregon: we had let our imaginations get overworked.

However, if the rains hadn't stopped, we wouldn't have been able to cross. We were lucky in that respect.

Ann's journal: Clouds threatened more rain most of the day, but always held off, and we even had bits of sun now and then. We hiked some high traverses that gave us marvelous views back to Cathedral and Mount Daniel. Coming down into the Surprise cirque we saw lots of marmots and huge blocks of white granite that contrasted sharply with patches of green meadow.

Our last climb of the day was over Trap Pass from which we could see our lake below—home for the night. The tarp is set up in a tiny little campsite, quite cozy. It is very cold tonight. I usually leave the foot end of my sleeping bag unzipped because my feet get so hot, but maybe tonight it will get zipped up all the way.

Lee's journal: I am impressed by the Alpine Lakes Wilderness. It is rugged and beautiful, a place to come back to for exploring and fishing.

We are now only eleven miles out of Stevens Pass. It hardly seems possible to be here, based on yesterday's storm. We had considered ending the hike and retreating to Salmon la Sac or Scenic, or hiking back to the Hyas Lake alternate, which would have lost us a day. Instead, everything went right, and now we are this close to Stevens Pass. Tomorrow, with no problems, we will be on our last major leg: Stevens Pass to Canada! We will be retracing the section I hiked in 1978, and, based on that experience, we could do it in just ten days! I am admittedly looking forward to the end of cold showers, struggling to stay warm and dry, and walking day after day.

Many miles still lie ahead. Each day's progress seems so tentative as our mood and outlook change with the weather and the hardships of the day.

SEPTEMBER 12

Log: 13 miles from Trap Lake to a tributary of Nason Creek. Clear skies, white fluffy clouds, no rain, no wind.

Lee's journal: The sky cleared last night and was starlit for the first time since Lizard Lake. We broke camp to a sunrise. What a good feeling to see the

Thunder Mountain in the morning sun.

Repacking at Stevens Pass.

sun coming up in an all-blue sky! A beautiful day to be hiking. We saw a couple of deer in a meadow shortly after starting out, and I had a hard time keeping up my pace since I was busy scanning the meadows and hillsides for more animals as we went along.

Ann's journal: We were on the trail by 7am—one of the earliest starts recently. Lots of ups and downs today—drop to a lake, climb to a pass, drop to a lake, climb to a pass. Lee has a sore toe and was not always right behind me on the "downs," but easily caught me on the "ups," as usual.

At last we topped the final ridge with Stevens Pass below us. Then it did seem actually within reach. At the Ranger Station, I found Tina Katzenberger out in her back yard squashing aluminum cans. She let us into her husband's office (he is the Stevens Pass Ranger) and we collected our supply boxes that I had left with her a couple of months earlier. Tina generously donated a couple of fresh peaches to our lunch. We devoured them, along with the can of chili and brown bread from our supply box.

Lee's journal: In the parking lot we met a couple who were setting out to hike to Stehekin, taking ten days. And as we were repacking, we also met the two guys and dog whose tracks we have been follow-

ing—one of these fellows is the same one we saw at
Cascade Locks! They had spent the night in Skykomish and were now anxious to be back on the trail
with the good weather. They had gotten pretty wet
during the rainstorm.

I called the folks from a pay phone at the pass.

Ann's journal: As Lee was in the phone booth, a
strange man came up and asked, "Do you know that
man in the phone booth?" I said, "Yes." And he
said, "Do you know he's dangerous?"

I scooched away from him a little bit, stared the
other way, and hoped that Lee would hurry; this guy
was obviously a nut.

But he looked at me and grinned and said, "I'm
Paul." Then it fell into place. Paul—Lee's friend
from the shipyard! I was glad Lee had told me about
him before this.

Lee's journal: Paul said that it was such nice weather
he took the day off and drove up to the pass to see
if we had come through yet. He took us down to
Skykomish for beer, root beer, milk, cinnamon rolls,
Cheetos, fudgesicles. A nice break from routine.

Back at Stevens Pass, we walked 2½ miles north
to a wide spot in the trail at a tributary of Nason
Creek, a total of thirteen miles for the day. Not
much of a camp, but it's flat and well-protected, with
convenient water. It is exciting to be on the north
side of Stevens Pass. We are within two weeks of
reaching Canada.

Ann's journal: We came into this supply point *on
schedule* at last! We have made up all of our "late"
days!

SEPTEMBER 13

Log: 15.7 miles from Nason Creek to Pear Lake. Clear skies changing to cloudy; cool with light wind.

Ann's journal: Lee was up before the alarm this morning, anxious to get going. On mornings when he is so enthusiastic to start hiking, he takes the

Frozen droplets of dew.

tarp down as I'm getting dressed, and it collapses
over my head when he pulls the stakes out. Grrrr!

This section to Stehekin has lots of ups and downs
that have me completely "psyched-out." A thousand
feet here, a thousand feet there, up and down. I
go slowly uphill, even though I try to maintain a
2mph pace. My pack is heavy and my back still
complains about it, after all these weeks.

Lee's journal: It would seem that after two months
of this, my body would be used to the load and
the miles and stop complaining. Not so! The only
difference is now we can keep going whereas before
we would need to take many rest stops.

I hope we can keep to our schedule and finish
on time—or maybe even a day early. We're going
to need a couple of days to unwind from this job
of hiking before we must face the everyday world.
It will be a shock to adjust to "normal" living again.

When this hike is done, I think I don't want to
hike for awhile—and then only in good weather!

Ann's journal: Although Lee passed through here
five years ago, he is seeing this country for the first
time, as it rained every day of his first trip. I hope
the weather gives him enough breaks so he can see
what he missed before.

Our camp at Pear Lake is quite snug, even smaller
than the little camp at Trap Lake a couple of nights

Sloan Peak.

ago. Right across the trail is a tumbling brook—I
just held the jug under a little waterfall to fill it up.
We are a ways up from the lake shore, out of the
wind that seems to funnel through down there.

Someone else has used this camp recently as there
are fresh-cut boughs padding the ground. We set up
camp right over them, and wondered what other
people would think if they saw our camp—would they
think *we* cut the boughs?

Made lots of pancakes for dinner tonight with
rice and chicken.

For quite awhile we had been having trouble with mice.
First they got into the garbage and made a mess of things for
several nights. We foiled them by hanging the garbage bag
from a tarp line. But they just took that as a challenge and
began coming right into the tarp to rummage through our
gear like vandals, skittering over our sleeping bags and shred-
ding the evening's tea bag.

Their antics got old after a very short time. At Pear
Lake, Lee had had *enough*, and when the mouse came around
to rattle the pots and pans for the thirty-seventh time, Lee
tried to pound it with his fist, and threw his cup and spoon
and the pot and whatever else was handy at it as it scampered
off into the night.

We knew that Stehekin, our next supply stop, had a small
store, and we planned delightedly how we would buy a mouse-
trap there and "do in" every mouse in the North Cascades.

SEPTEMBER 14

Log: 15.6 miles from Pear Lake to Kid Pond. Heavy clouds blowing
in from southwest.

Ann's journal: This morning we woke up almost
socked in. Climbing up out of the lake basin to
Frozen Finger Gap, we were dripped on from the
trees, and blown on by an icy wind, but the day
gradually improved. I feel as though we're on
"borrowed time" to have a whole day without rain.
Sure makes a difference in how the spirit accepts life.

On Kodak Peak we found an abandoned pack
that had a brand new pair of boots in it, among
other things. We certainly couldn't carry it with
us, but we retrieved it from down the slope and
set it up by the trail. We speculate it might have

Our little camp at Kid Pond.

fallen from a horse party we saw earlier.

Lee's journal: Spent about half an hour fishing after lunch at Lake Sally Ann. Out of several strikes, I hooked two and landed one, which I released.

Ann's journal: We met a couple of kids hiking from the Suiattle down to Stevens Pass. They had put in a hard day yesterday, they told us, covering ten miles. Later, Lee commented, "Gee, we do one of their 'hard' days before lunch!" Our perspective certainly has changed.

Lee's journal: We had planned on camping at Indian Pass, but a group of six men and eleven horses had set up a good-sized hunting camp. We visited with them for a few minutes and asked if theirs was the pack we had found on Kodak Peak. No, they weren't missing any packs, they said.

We continued to camp at Kid Pond. Although it's just a wide spot on the trail, it's adequate for the tarp. The water is marginal, but we've had worse to drink.

Ann's journal: If we don't get rain tonight, we'll be in the middle of a damp, drippy cloud by morning, at the very least! We're on the side of a mountain at 5300 feet, with clouds swirling all around, and the peak above us already shrouded in thick fog.

Lee's journal: We had a feast at dinner: rice with tomato sauce, and spaghetti with mung bean sprouts (that Ann grows in her pack), and vanilla pudding *and* coffee cake. For a second dessert we had a piece of Hershey bar. And for a third dessert, we'll have chocolate pudding with tea.

We've decided not to take a layover day at Kennedy Hot Springs, but to take it in Stehekin instead. We may not even take the side trip to Kennedy at all, since it will certainly be crowded.

SEPTEMBER 15

Log: 15.6 miles from Kid Pond to Glacier Creek. Cloudless in morning, wisps of cloud by noon, overcast and threatening by evening.

Lee's journal: We woke to clear skies and headed out in good spirits because of the weather. A great day to be alive! I hoped all the animals would make it safely through this opening day of the high hunt. It would be a shame to die on such a pretty day.

Glacier Peak from Red Pass.

Keeping the log up-to-date at Glacier Creek.

Ann's journal: My breakfasts have been "wearing off" about 10:30 each morning, which leaves me with a rumbling stomach until lunch. It gets pretty noisy. Occasionally Lee will stop and say with surprise, "What's that noise?" but it's just my stomach.

This morning I had *two* breakfasts because I have a couple of extras, and that plus a few blueberries kept the rumbling down.

It's a good thing we camped at Kid Pond last night instead of going another mile to the next camp, as this morning we discovered the next camp was occupied. And so was the next camp at Reflection Pond, and the one after that below White Pass! We felt lucky to have had such a nice spot, although it certainly didn't look like much when we got there. There's something about putting up the tarp that makes the tiniest or brushiest or rockiest place seem like home.

Lee's journal: On the way up to Red Pass we met two hikers going our way who had stopped on the trail. They pointed out a bear halfway across the next sidehill and said they weren't certain what to do now. We assured them there was nothing to worry about; these bears will run when they see you, and if it would make them feel better, we'd go first.

They gladly let us pass, and we hoped we were doing the right thing! Not sure where the bear went; he was probably simply engrossed in his blueberry patch.

At Red Pass we dropped our packs and climbed to a high point. The view was great! We could see Rainier, Glacier Peak, and all of the surrounding country.

Ann's journal: We stopped for lunch at the Hot Springs trail junction, and were joined by several grey jays. When I saw that one was eyeing my granola bar, I held out a piece and he flew right to my hand for it. Lee had never seen the jays do that before, so he had fun holding out a piece for them, too.

Then we had a 1300-foot climb to reach our camp here—huff, puff—and we staggered in about 3:45, making it a 16-mile day. We heated water for a bath, which I needed as I fell earlier in the day on a muddy stretch and landed head downhill, with the pack pinning my arms and camera into the mud—couldn't get up! It happened so fast I couldn't remember what I'd done to end up there.

We're up high enough that we'll have daylight longer than usual this evening. And we'll also probably have frost in the morning, as we did at our last camp. It sure is getting cold. Lee had the foresight to switch to his heavyweight wool pants at Cascade Locks. I'm still using my lightweight ones, and berating myself. I may have to break out the long underwear to stay warm.

SEPTEMBER 16

Log: 17.7 miles from Glacier Creek to Vista Creek. Moderately miserable weather with rain and sleet, cold, and strong wind on exposed ridges.

Lee's journal: Happy birthday, Darren! Thought of you many times today.

> *Ann's journal:* I hope Darren thought of his dad in
> all the excitement of turning eight, because his dad
> was thinking of him. We've been away from our
> families for two months now, and really feel ex-
> cluded by the special occasions that fly by.

Leaving Glacier Creek at 7:15 the next morning, we hiked
18 miles through cold rain and sleet. I had been fretting
about the tremendous elevation gains and losses we would experience while rounding Glacier Peak. Fire Creek Pass, Vista
Ridge and Suiattle Pass loomed before me like dragons.

But today we crossed Fire Creek Pass and ascended Vista
Ridge—both before lunch, even! These high spots could have
given us spectacular views, but we were socked in. Lashed
with wind and rain, our vision hampered by fog, we rounded
Dolly Vista after lunch and finally trotted down toward
Vista Creek.

Our trail log noted that "this night's camp is the first
one we came to . . . has mice." We saw several parties of
hunters on horseback, and several other hikers, including the
local Wilderness Ranger. We "leapfrogged" on the trail with
a fellow from Boston who was hiking through the Glacier
Peak Wilderness.

> *Lee's journal:* Took only a few pictures today; just
> too wet to keep the camera out. Only two days
> before we reach Stehekin! I can hardly wait.
>
> Ann has a fire of sorts going and is drying some
> socks. She *hates* wet clothes!

SEPTEMBER 17

Log: 17.5 miles from Vista Creek to Hemlock Camp on Agnes Creek.
Cold. Rain and snow.

After more rain during the night, we set off to slay my
last dragon—Suiattle Pass.

> *Ann's journal:* It was cold and rainy this morning,
> and I knew the brush along the trail would be
> sopping, so as usual I put on my gaiters to hike in.
> The zippers are now so jammed with mud that I
> broke one of them trying to force it. I would have
> taken them both off and hiked without them, but
> Lee reminded me it would be wet and brushy, and
> told me to safety-pin the broken zipper and *wear*
> them. So I did.

Lee's journal: At the Vista Creek bridge we ran into the fellow from Boston again, who was sharing a camp with a young man named Scott. Scott had started at Manning Park and was heading for Mount Hood. He told us that in the Big Storm of September 10—just a week ago—he had been camped in four inches of snow in the North Cascades. He gave us information about Stehekin, and recommended their bakery. Asked us if we would say "hi" to Tammy and Lou at the bakery for him.

As we headed up to Suiattle Pass, we met several parties of hikers and hunters on horseback who were coming out because of the bad weather and snow.

Ann's journal: Oh, the miles were endless and the switchbacks went on and on. Near the top of the Pass we had rain, sleet, snow and fog. Instead of winding in and out of sidehills on the new, re-routed PCT, we chose the more direct old route down Agnes Creek. Still in snow, we turned off into the Agnes

Snow on Suiattle Pass.

Creek route, marked, "Trail abandoned."

Lee slipped and fell at one slippery stream crossing—soaked his boots and socks, and got his gloves wet. He wrung out his socks and put rain pants on to help warm him up.

Lee's journal: I bruised a foot and twisted my knee in the fall; hope I'll be okay to hike into Stehekin. We're only twelve miles away.

It has turned very cold. I could adapt to that alright if the rain and clouds would go away. It's one thing to have cold with blue skies and sun, and quite another to have cold with rain and clouds.

Hemlock Camp was spacious. Being the only souls there, we had our pick of sites in the open forest beside the creek.

Although we were always careful to keep tidy camps, this night we experienced the worst mouse attack of the entire trip. Mice in our packs, mice running the tarp cords like rats on a ship, mice scampering over our sleeping bags—mice in my *hair!* In desperation, I slept zipped up in my bivvy bag.

SEPTEMBER 18 and 19

Log: 12 miles from Hemlock Camp to High Bridge. Cold with snow and rain. Layover in Stehekin on the 19th.

In the morning, we surveyed the damage. Lee's fishing-pole-holder was chewed to shreds, and one of my pack pockets had a neat slice chewed right through it. We were furious at the mice.

Lee's journal: Awoke at Hemlock Camp to see snow falling! We couldn't believe it would be snowing at only 3500 feet! We set out at a good pace so we could get to High Bridge in hopes of catching an early-afternoon bus into Stehekin. We had snow and rain most of the way.

In our trail log, we commented, "The 'official' PCT joins the unmaintained route just south of camp. One might be inclined to think that the official route *would* be maintained, but it is just as bad—or worse—as the old unmaintained trail. Bridges are broken, trees are down, brush is a problem; it's generally a crummy trail."

As we dropped in elevation, the snow changed to rain. We were cold, and soaked from the brush, and irritated with the condition of the PCT through here. We checked the

Lake Chelan and the North Cascades.

shuttle bus schedule when we arrived at the High Bridge Guard Station, only to learn that we had missed the mid-day bus by just an hour, and we had *five hours* to wait for the next one.

> *Lee's journal:* As we put on heavier clothes and wrung out our socks, we hoped someone going by would give us a ride. In a short while Park Service Ranger Tom Evans did come by. He was out driving the road to see if anyone was stranded, like us, since the bus schedule had changed just today. It really made our day to arrive in Stehekin by 1pm.

Coming into Stehekin felt like entering the Emerald City of Oz. People, cars, hustle and bustle—and the rain had stopped! The first thing we did, after thanking Tom for the ride, was to head for Karl Warner's bakery stand on the boat dock. Karl was selling fresh whole-wheat cinnamon rolls, cookies, brownies and bread. I know I had at least one of everything, and Lee went back for seconds! We arranged to have a pie baked for us in the morning.

The next order of business was to get a room at the lodge, and then to check the mouse-trap supply at the store. We weren't impressed by either the room or the store.

> *Ann's journal:* This room was by far the most ex-

pensive we have had on the whole trip—$58 for one night, complete with dripping faucet, too-small shower curtain, power that shuts off for fifteen minutes every morning at 7—and a resident mouse, just when we thought we would be *free* of them!

The little store had only a few items (no mouse-traps), although we hid our disappointment and managed to spend $40 on groceries there.

Our room does give us space to spread out our things and dry them completely, which we haven't been able to do since Snoqualmie Pass. The little kitchen gives us freedom from backpacking menus.

Lee's journal: We ate dinner at the lodge, and met Bruce, Greg, and Mike, PCT hikers from California who started out at the Mexican border last spring. They came into Stehekin today all the way from Miner's Ridge, hurrying out of the snow and rain as we did.

It turns out that we were behind them all through Oregon and Washington, and we've been reading their comments in trail registers and signpost notes all along the way. At Snoqualmie Pass they took a few days off, where we passed them. They told us the two-guys-with-dog we've been following are also here. We talked with the three for some time after dinner. They, too, have had mouse problems!

Ann's journal: We spent our layover day very leisure-ly. First we walked over to the Post Office to collect our supply boxes. We each got letters, and I got a package of dried fruit from the Clarks in California! It's nice to be remembered by friends "out there." Then we walked to the bakery to pick up our fresh Stehekin blackberry pie. It wasn't quite ready when we arrived, so we sat, drank some tea, and talked with Tammy. We told her "hi" from Scott.

Lee's journal: After getting back to the lodge, we bought more cinnamon rolls, and soaked in the hot tub. Mike and Bruce came to join us. It's interest-ing to compare trail experiences. Hearing them tell it, we probably are better prepared and staying drier than they are. Perhaps Ann and I are doing better in the gloom of the rain than it seems.

Today is a beautiful day. We are torn between staying another day to relax, or continuing. The rest of the PCTers will be heading out tomorrow, to get the most miles in while the weather holds.

Our pie is very good—as good as Ann or I can make ourselves, which is not usually the case with ordinary bakery pies. But this is no ordinary bakery!

I hope tomorrow will bring good weather. It sure looked dismal when we checked the weather report today, and were told that at least six inches of snow have fallen at 6000 feet—the rest of our trail spends a lot of time over 6000 feet! We will continue regardless, since there are "escape routes" we can take in an emergency.

In the Bridge Creek drainage.

Golden larches in the high country.

SEPTEMBER 20

Log: 12.7 miles (Ann thinks it's 15 miles) from Bridge Creek to a mile east of Rainy Pass. Frost this morning.

Lee's journal: We're on our final section! We were up at 6am to finish off the pie and have breakfast, and to catch the 8am shuttle bus back up to the PCT. It was exciting to set off today under sunny and warm blue skies. The rumor is that it may stay this way for a day or so. The locals on the bus said the temperature last night was 36, so where we'll be camping tonight could get to freezing.

Mike, Greg and Bruce also left today with us. We thought the two-with-dog were going today, too, but when the bus went by their camp, their tents were still set up.

Ann's journal: Hiking up Bridge Creek, Lee dropped

his camera case over a cliff. Disaster. To get to it, he had to continue on the trail until he could cut around to the bottom of the cliff, and then scramble through brush and boulders, searching. I stayed at the top to guide him, and after some shouting back and forth over the roar of the river he found it.

Lee's journal: We were carrying fresh bread, cheese, cinnamon rolls, dried fruit and Sharon's cookies, so we had a big lunch to help reduce the packs.

I had hoped we would be able to camp at State Creek, where Dennis and I did in '78, but the trail had been recently re-routed—too recent even for the guidebook to cover it.

Our trail log noted: "We are camped off-trail to the south just before the trail reaches the meadow and parking lot on Highway 20. There's lots of firewood, water handy, and level ground. Saw one party of hunters with eight deer."

Lee's journal: We are both trying not to think too much about the end of the hike. Our day-to-day world of just the two of us for the past two and a half months will end and we will face a difficult adjustment to the "normal" world.

SEPTEMBER 21

Log: 16.6 miles from Rainy Pass to Willis Camp. No rain! Blue sky!

From Granite Pass, the PCT cuts below Tower Mountain.

Lee's journal: We awoke to clear sky and had a beautiful day. We ran into snow part-way up to Cutthroat Pass that lasted off and on until well below Methow Pass; in some places the drifts were a foot deep on the trail. We had hoped to push hard today, but with sore feet we stopped here for 16½ miles. We really wanted to get farther before the weather changes. From the way the snow is still piled up here, we don't want to be around when the next storm comes through.

I found hiking through a foot of snow pretty tough going, although nothing seemed to slow Lee down. Way up high at 6000 feet it was *cold*, the larches were turning golden, and the open country above timberline was fantastic.

Ann's journal: Another campfire tonight. It's nice to be able to sit around the fire like this in good weather, with nothing desperately in need of drying.

With the nice weather, we had not even set up the tarp since leaving Stehekin.

Azurite Peak from Grasshopper Pass.

High, open country north of Harts Pass.

SEPTEMBER 22

Log: 15.7 miles from Willis Camp to Harts Pass. Cold. No rain, blue sky, some wind at passes.

> *Ann's journal:* Last night I had sore feet that didn't recover this morning, and today I took aspirin for the first time in quite a while. My right ankle is really giving me a problem. Why does this have to happen so close to Canada?

The trail along the Methow River was lined with frost in the morning. As we turned into the Brush Creek drainage and climbed up into the sunlight, the frost along the overgrown path melted and soaked our legs.

> *Ann's journal:* Today's views were spectacular. In all directions, we saw only mountains and glaciers as far as the horizon. Our third beautiful day in a row. We met some vacationing hikers from Maine today who told us the weather prediction is for the next storm to move in on Saturday (today's Thursday). We walked the road into Harts Pass campground to avoid snow on northfacing slopes. Lee went ahead and was at the campground long before me.

> *Lee's journal:* We're sharing the campground with the

three guys we left Stehekin with—hope they're quiet!

SEPTEMBER 23

Log: 22.5 miles from Harts Pass to Mountain Home Basin. Cold, with strong wind from the southwest.

We awoke early to a very pink sunrise with haze and clouds off to the west. As we left Harts Pass, the sun was just coming over the eastern ridge.

We gained elevation rapidly, staying well above 6000 feet for miles. We knew we should be able to see Mount Baker— the last of our guiding volcanoes—but just which mountain *was* it in all that hazy sea of peaks? Used to seeing Mount Baker only from the west, I couldn't for the life of me pick it out from the other side!

After dropping to 5000 feet to cross Holman Pass, we gained elevation again to put us back between 6000 and 7000 feet. Our planned camp was to have been at a spring in a huge basin southwest of Holman Peak. But when we arrived at the spot, it was only mid-afternoon. The sun was out, the air was cool and brisk, and views of the high peaks of the Pasayten were grand. We decided to continue.

Across Rock Pass, under the sheer east face of Powder Mountain, up to 6600-foot Woody Pass, below Three Fool's

Views of the Pasayten peaks were grand.

Peak, until in a couple of hours we rounded a shoulder of Lakeview Ridge and came to a halt to survey the scene below us.

An expansive open bowl, bright red and gold from autumn leaves, fell away in a series of benches to a stream bed a thousand feet below. Clumps of trees on the upper benches offered shelter. Patches of marsh indicated water. To camp there meant we would have to drop a couple of hundred feet, but it looked so inviting we didn't mind the elevation loss.

Expansive Mountain Home basin.

Descending on an obscure side trail and then roaming cross-country, we found a perfect spot. It seems others had thought so, too, as we found a small sign at our chosen spot which read: "Mountain Home Camp, '54. K. Thompson, G Griffin."

We wondered who those people were and how they happened to have carved a sign that remained almost thirty years later for us to find. (A year later, after a story about our hike had appeared in Signpost Magazine, I received a letter from Herb Rudolph of Pendleton, Oregon, who had known K. Thompson and G. Griffin. "Ken Thompson was a trail foreman when trail maintenance was a profession in the Forest Service," Mr. Rudolph wrote. "George Griffin was a member

Off comes the pack at Mountain Home Camp.

of Ken's crew....Ken had a fierce pride in the trail system
...You will find other of his signs in the Pasayten country.")

Adding up our mileage for the day, we were surprised
to total 22½ miles from Harts Pass—the longest day of our
trip. Only seventeen miles remained to Manning Park. We
decided to do it all the next day. Mountain Home would be
our last night out. With clouds hovering in the western sky,
we set up the tarp one last time, and hoped the weather
would hold *one more day.*

> *Lee's journal:* An exposed camp and possibly some
> weather moving in; however, a very beautiful spot.

Several times that night we awoke to watch a beautiful
full moon make its way across the sky.

SEPTEMBER 24

**Log: 16.8 miles from Mountain Home to Manning Park Lodge. Cold
in morning; warm in afternoon.**

Up with the dawn, we went through our routine of
breakfast, tarp down, and packing that had become so familiar
over the many weeks. We were on our way shortly after 7am,
climbing out of the basin back to the PCT.

> *Ann's journal:* I have had so much trouble with my
> feet swelling every night that putting on my boots

has become an ordeal. I struggle and struggle with them until they go on—there's no choice: they *must* go on. It is the most horrible part of every day. Today the boot struggle had to take place one last time, and I *won* for one more time.

We had to climb ¼-mile up a steep slope to get back to the PCT, but once on the trail the going was easy and within a mile or two we had climbed to our high point of about 7100 feet just as the sun was coming over the high ridges. What a sight with mountains around in every direction—certainly too much to take in all at once. We both were much impressed with such grandeur. We positively identified Mount Baker again—it's different from the peak we positively identified as Mount Baker yesterday.

After soaking up the sights, we dropped off the ridge to Hopkins Lake, leaving the high country behind. We felt exhilarated at being in such wild country, and both happy and sad that our journey was ending. After many more miles we reached Monument 78 on the United States/Canada border, which had been our goal for so long.

Walking into the little clearing that held the border monument, we took off our packs and spent many minutes there. We had lunch and took photographs and added our names on a slip of paper to the informal "trail register."

Mountains in every direction.

Lee and Monument 78—the United States/Canada border.

Posing by the PCT sign near Monument 78.

Seven miles still remained from the Monument to Manning Park Lodge.

> *Lee's journal:* We hadn't recovered from yesterday's long mileage, but the desire to reach the end of the trail kept us going. Hiking downhill on the Windy Joe Road was hard on the feet! On this road, we met a couple from New Zealand just starting out. They were headed for Mount Rainier and didn't appear too well prepared—no maps or guidebook! We told them where a good campspot was.

About 3 that afternoon, we stepped out of the forest beside Canada's Highway 3. The cars whizzing by with British Columbia license plates emphasized that we were actually there—in Manning Park—and after a short walk down the highway, we reached the Lodge.

We felt both exhilaration and relief as we trudged into the lobby of the Lodge. One last supply box awaited us here —not food and maps this time, but "civilized" clothes: jeans and shirts that were fresh and clean. The box had been personally delivered by my father earlier in the summer when members of my family had driven through Manning Park.

We had been looking forward to spending a day or two at Manning Park before we returned home, but the Lodge was in the process of closing down until new managers could be found.

> *Lee's journal:* We were disappointed that the dining room was no longer open, so we had dinner in the cafeteria. It wasn't the celebration meal we had thought about.

> *Ann's journal:* After we checked into a room at the Lodge, I *took my boots off!* Since the Lodge is closing, we didn't find the remaining facilities worth staying a couple of days for. Lee has been saying that we ought to visit Victoria.

> *Lee's journal:* Two buses a day come through the Park for Vancouver, one at 2am and one at 1pm. We'll spend the night and catch the afternoon bus.

We kept reminding ourselves that we were really in Canada, had really finished our thousand-mile walk. And not only that—we had finished two days ahead of our planned schedule! 'Way back in Oregon it had seemed as though we didn't stand a chance of making up our lost days. We had surprised ourselves by catching up to and passing our schedule.

> *Lee's journal:* We were awakened by party noise
> from a weekend convention. The noise kept me
> awake until the small hours, and I spent part of
> the time packing my things and considering catch-
> ing the 2am bus! We've added another to our list
> of Places Not To Camp: hotels with conventions.
>
> During the night we kept the window open for
> air. After two and a half months of living out of
> doors, I wonder how I will adapt to a stuffy office
> space again.

THE JOURNEY ENDS...

The next morning we spent relaxing and waiting for our bus. We visited again with the three fellows from California, who hiked in that morning. Seeing us in our "tourist clothes" of jeans and sneakers, they said with some disappointment, "Gee, you guys don't look like Trail People anymore!"

It was true. Gone were the nylon shorts and grubby shirts, the wool socks and heavy boots we had worn day after day in all kinds of weather. We were beginning to transform ourselves from adventurers into our ordinary selves.

It turned out that the couple from New Zealand had camped at the same spot as the three men had. We had hoped that would happen, as the New Zealanders needed a lot of information, and the three men ended up giving them their copy of the PCT guidebook.

One of the men was returning to a carpentry job in Monterrey; the other two were going to hike some more in California before the season ended.

We said goodbye to them and boarded our bus.

> *Lee's journal:* Making our way to Victoria is a
> new adventure, and helps ease the letdown of
> ending the Pacific Crest Trail.

Looking out the windows of the huge vehicle, we had fun letting ourselves be amazed at how rapidly we covered ground. In only a few hours, we were in downtown Vancouver—why, it would have taken us *days* to walk the distance!

> *Lee's journal:* In Vancouver, we bought bus tickets
> for Victoria and got a bite to eat at the cafeteria
> there, then got in line for the bus. A football

game had just ended and the station was crowded
with people waiting for the bus back to Victoria.
It was quite a shock for us to be packed in like
sardines.

We didn't have a place to stay in Victoria, so I
collected some brochures on the ferry and we picked
a likely hotel.

Ann's journal: From the bus depot in Victoria, we
had to walk through dark, strange streets with our
packs to reach the hotel. We ended up with a
unique, two-story room that had a great view.

Lee's journal: It costs more than we should have
spent, but it puts a nice finish on our journey.

One of the high spots of our time in Victoria was finding
a Dutch bakery and, after trying out a few tidbits, buying an
entire three-layer chocolate cake which we gleefully carted off
to a park bench on the harbor. In a short time, we had devoured the entire cake. We nearly made ourselves ill, but it helped
to take the edge off the craving for sweets and pastries we had!

On our second night in Victoria, we had a lasagna dinner in
a nice restaurant. Even though Lee was still hungry, he was
too self-conscious to order a *second* dinner there. Instead,
we went to another restaurant where he had a second plate
of lasagna, and we topped off the evening with hot-fudge
sundaes at still a *third* restaurant!

We carted our cake off to a park bench on the harbor.

Besides eating, we also enjoyed strolling through the streets—no packs on, no concerns about where to camp and where the next water was. We visited the impressive museum and the botanical gardens.

Late in the afternoon of September 27th, we boarded the *Princess Marguerite*, the passenger liner between Seattle and Victoria, and started the last leg of the trip.

Finishing off the journal on the deck of the Princess Marguerite.

Ann's journal: Looking back, it certainly doesn't seem like very long since we started on July 17th to where we ended on September 24th. Living out of a backpack became a normal and accepted way of life. We certainly had rough spots, but given a little time, or rest, or food and warmth, the irritation and frustration seemed to dissolve. We did pretty well traveling together. In spite of some hardships and absolutely miserable times, we did have many,

many nice camps and beautiful views. The feeling
of setting up camp with a friend at the close of a
beautiful day can't be beat.

Lee's journal: I want to collect my thoughts about
the trip before they grow too clouded. I still don't
know the answer to "why this trip?" Maybe I just
wanted to do something different; maybe I wanted
the challenge. Whatever—I'm glad I did it.
  Some of the memories can be recorded only by
making a list:

  -cold showers, sometimes with 40-degree spring
   water, and once with snow
  -watching the weather: hoping it wouldn't rain,
   being disappointed when it did; walking in it,
   living in it, with everything damp
  -sleeping on hard ground
  -the chill coming right through the ensolite pad
  -never being warm enough toward the end of
   the hike
  -Ann's struggle with her boots
  -my feet aching
  -damp boots; and putting on *wet* socks morning
   after morning
  -mud
  -wind coming around the edge of the tarp no
   matter how I put it up
  -mice running over me at night
  -views hidden by rain and fog and mist
  -expensive food and rooms at resorts
  -being hungry a lot of the time
  -drinking water from potholes
  -mosquitoes and flies
  -going downhill with sore feet

There were good things, too:
  -reaching camp in the afternoon and putting
   our house together
  -mint cake
  -accomplishment as the miles built up; seeing
   our progress on the map
  -views when the weather co-operated
  -rice with beef and garlic, and hotcakes

-seeing the animals along the trail (except the
 mice)
-surviving the Big Storm of September 10th, and
 snow, and other rigors
-freedom to do as I wanted
-pudding and tea before bed
-the feeling of having done something not many
 people do
-the satisfaction of walking into Manning Park

The trip has shown me just how little a person
needs for survival. Our society has convinced us
we need too many *things*.

The hike has also given me the feeling that I can
survive if I take problems a step at a time. I made
it through the hardships of the Trail; certainly I can
make it through the problems of modern life.

The hike is over. I will be a better person because of having done it. If I can hike a thousand
miles of the Pacific Crest Trail, I can do anything I
set my mind to!